Move, *and* I Will Move

How the Great Church Builder
Taught Me Step by Step

By
Arvid Kingsriter
with Lynne Jonell

Move and I Will Move Copyright © 2006 by Arvid Kingsriter.

All rights reserved. No part of this book may be reproduced in any form, except for the inclusion of brief quotations in a review, without written permission from the author.

ISBN 0-9762461-1-2
Library of Congress Control Number 2006900143
Cover art copyright © 2006 by Lynne Jonell. All rights reserved.
Photographs courtesy of North Central University archives and the author.

All scripture quotations, unless otherwise indicated, are taken from the Holy Bible, New Kings James Version®. Copyright © 1982 by Thomas Nelson, Inc. Used by permission. All rights reserved.

Scripture quotations marked (NASB) are taken from the New American Standard Bible®, copyright © 1960, 1962, 1963, 1968, 1971, 1972, 1973, 1975, 1977, 1995 by The Lockman Foundation. Used by permission. All rights reserved.

Scripture quotations marked (LB) are taken from the Living Bible, copyright © 1971 by Tyndale House Publishers, Inc. Used by permission. All rights reserved.

Scripture quotations marked (NIV) are taken from the Holy Bible, New International Version®, NIV®, copyright © 1973, 1978, 1984 by International Bible Society. Used by permission of Zondervan. All rights reserved.

Scripture quotations marked (KJV) are taken from the Holy Bible, King James Version.

Some scripture quotations are taken from The Message by Eugene H. Peterson, copyright © 1993, 1994, 1995, 1996, 2000, 2001, 2002. Used by permission of NavPress Publishing Group.

Additional copies of this book are available by mail from:
University Bookstore, North Central University
910 Elliot Avenue / Minneapolis, Minnesota 55404
Send e-mail inquiries to bookstore@northcentral.edu
or call (612) 343-7887.

Printed in the USA by Morris Publishing
3212 East Highway 30, Kearney, Nebraska 68847
1-800-650-7888

Published by: North Central University Press
910 Elliot Avenue / Minneapolis, Minnesota 55404
612-343-4200 or 1-800-289-6222 / www.northcentral.edu

*With enduring gratitude,
remembering those who guided me
in my formative years, especially:*

*Oscar Klingsheim, who taught me how to become a Christian
so that I might be able to lead others to Christ;
R. D. E. Smith, who showed me how to pioneer churches
so that God's kingdom would expand more rapidly;
and Ivan O. Miller, who was patient with me
during my years of development as a faculty member
at North Central.*

*These men taught me more by the life they lived
than by what they said.*

*And with love I also dedicate this book
to my dear wife Marian,
and our beloved children and grandchildren;
with special thanks to my daughter Lynne,
who gave so much of her time and energy
to make this book a reality;
and to Jac Perrin, who encouraged me
to write a record of my life and ministry.*

*Many thanks, too, to the leadership of North Central University
and the Minnesota District Council of the Assemblies of God
who have so kindly given their support to this project.*

Contents

Foreword
Introductory Note on Name Changes
Preface

1. The Call of God 11
2. Measuring Up 19
3. Learning to Pray..27
4. When You Make Up Your Mind, Let Me Know 33
5. Starting at the Bottom 41
6. Compel Them to Come In...51
7. Faith and Personal Finances 59
8. Building a Church on Faith 67
9. Leadership Lessons 79
10. The Latter Rain Crisis 87
11. Testing Prophecy and Guidance 95
12. Casino Revival 105
13. Facing Criticism..115
14. Work and Lots of It 123
15. Giving Up Control 133
16. Caution Signs 149
17. Move, and I Will Move 161
18. I Will Get You Ready 173
19. Singing in the Dark..181
20. Changing of the Guard 195
21. Pressing On 205

Foreword

Outside our family circle, there are a few people who cross our paths over the course of our lifetime, and dramatically impact and shape us. When I think of such individuals, Arvid Kingsriter is one of the first names that come to my mind.

Our relationship began when I was a junior in college and he served as my professor and class advisor. This influence continued as I left college and moved to the Iron Range to pastor a church. In my mind, Arvid Kingsriter set the bar for leadership, for integrity, for prayer, for faith and vision, and for excellence. The way he did things influenced how I did things.

As pastor of a flagship church in the Minnesota District of the Assemblies of God, Arvid blazed a clear trail for young ministers to follow. He was not just concerned about his place of ministry; he was concerned about the kingdom of God. His actions spoke louder than his words.

When I came to the District Office sixteen years ago, Arvid threw his weight behind me. Because of the high esteem his fellow ministers had for him, his support gave me a credibility that would have taken me years to attain on my own—for when Arvid Kingsriter spoke on any subject, people listened.

Sometimes we wonder what makes a great man great. In writing *Move, and I Will Move*, Arvid has opened the door on his life and given us some of the answers.

Clarence St. John, Superintendent
Minnesota District Council of the Assemblies of God

Introductory Note on Name Changes

Throughout the span of this book, the names of institutions mentioned have changed to reflect their changing status, purpose, or demographic makeup. To assist the reader, we offer the following:

North Central University
- 1929: Established as North Central Bible Institute
- 1957: Name changed to North Central Bible College
- 1998: Name changed to North Central University

Cedar Valley Church
- 1953: Established as Bloomington Assembly of God
- 2002: Name changed to Cedar Valley Church upon addition of a second campus in Eagan

Lake Geneva Christian Center
- 1927: Lake Geneva Bible Camp
- 1995: Name changed to Lake Geneva Christian Center

Christ's Church
- 1924: Called the Minneapolis Gospel Tabernacle when F. J. Lindquist becomes its pastor
- 1977: Name changed to Christ's Church

Preface

Not long ago I was talking with a colleague of mine, Dr. Glen Menzies, when the subject of mortality came up. One of our elder ministers had just passed away and we were both rather sad. Not only would we miss this man as a leader and a friend, but we also felt that our Pentecostal Movement would be diminished, since we no longer had access to his wisdom and expertise.

It was at this point in the conversation that Glen said, "Somebody should do something about this. The history of our district, our school, and our churches will die out with these guys if we don't record it soon!"

His words got stuck in my heart.

And so I called Rev. Arvid Kingsriter, and asked if he would write his story for the sake of posterity. He hesitated at first, but as I pressed, he finally agreed to give it a shot.

Pastor Arvid is a naturally gifted storyteller. But as he began to write, we realized that we were overlooking a wonderful asset: a daughter who is a professional writer! Lynne Jonell helped us tell the story of her father, Arvid Kingsriter, and so many other pioneers of the faith in the Assemblies of God of Minnesota.

I believe that with this book we have rescued a great treasure. I now sleep better, knowing that we honor God by remembering His mighty deeds done in the days past.

Jac Perrin, Senior Pastor
Eden Prairie Assembly of God

1
The Call of God

"...Who has saved us, and called us with a holy calling, not according to our works, but according to His own purpose and grace which was given to us in Christ Jesus before time began..."
2 Timothy 1:9

"How did God call you, Arvid?"

The question was directed at a nineteen year old kid sitting on a hard folding chair in Miller Hall. It was February of 1941, my senior year at North Central Bible Institute, and my questioners were about to make a decision that would impact the rest of my life. Should they ordain me—or not?

Facing me around three sides of a long table were presbyters with such names as F. J. Lindquist, Ivan O. Miller, Emil Balliet, Russell Olson, Bill Katter—pioneers in the Pentecostal Movement, giants in the Assemblies of God, men I greatly respected.

I felt very small. Who was I to face these men of faith and say God had called me? I was a farm boy, without even a high school diploma. I had had no encounter with a burning bush, like Moses. God had not spoken to me in the night, like the boy Samuel.

Well, not with an audible voice, anyway. And yet He *had* spoken to me in the night, I remembered. Not with words, not with anything so clear, but with an overwhelming impression upon my heart.

I was just nine, walking between the barn and the house one starry night, when I stopped by the old windmill and looked up. Stars are very bright in the country, and I decided to count them all. But I soon gave up.

How many there were! How vast and distant the stars, and how powerful the hand that had thrown them into space! My will just melted before Him. I looked up at the brilliant heavens and felt an inner surge of conviction that the one who created the stars must have created me with a purpose in mind. He had plans for me, amazing though it seemed. And so I prayed, "God, if You can use me, I'm willing to serve you."

But was this a call to the ministry? I did not think so at the time. In fact, at age nine I had yet to feel entirely sure of my salvation. I could hardly become a minister without knowing I was saved, could I?

Of one fact I was certain, and the stars had made it plain. There was a great yawning gulf between my small and inadequate self, and the greatness and power of God; and I was completely incapable of bridging that vast chasm.

Faithful Parents

Unbeknownst to me, my parents, Albert and Lillian Kingsriter, were feeling a spiritual lack as well. They were godly people, who raised their five boys with daily Bible readings and prayer around the kitchen table. But when I was ten years old, they began to feel that the German Evangelical Church they attended was drifting far from biblical principles.

They kept reading things in the Bible that were not being taught in their church. Could God really heal people? Did God fill people with His Spirit? That is what the Bible said.

From left to right: Albert, Harland, Delmar, Orrin, George, Lillian, and Arvid Kingsriter.

"Is it true?" Dad asked our pastor. "And if it is, why don't you preach it?"

The Call of God

"I believe it is true," said our pastor. "But if I spoke about it from the pulpit, I might lose my job!"

My parents did not want their children to grow up in a church where the pastor believed one thing, but preached another. They wanted us to learn the truth, so they began to have church in our own home with just the family.

Soon after this, Dad developed an open sore on his neck. It kept draining and would not heal, no matter what the doctors did. The medical wisdom of that time called it 'tuberculosis of the skin', and the doctors said there was nothing they could do. Because of the discharge, Dad had to put a bandage over it to keep the dust and dirt of farming from getting into the infected and open sore.

My father heard about a healing service at a place called Lake Geneva Bible Camp, and went. When the evangelist, Charles Price, laid hands on my father's head and prayed for him, Dad felt an overwhelming sense of the power of God, and his knees gave way beneath him. He lay prostrate on the platform for about 45 minutes. He told us later that the Spirit of God seemed to completely envelop him. On the 50 mile trip home, he was so happy that he couldn't stop singing!

The next morning after chores, Dad went to the mirror on the wall to put a fresh bandage on the sore, as usual. He took off the old bandage and suddenly cried out, "I've been healed! I'VE BEEN HEALED!!" I ran to look, along with the rest of my family, and we saw that the sore was no longer open and running with fluid, but was covered with new, pink skin, just like the skin of a baby!

Dad exclaimed, "I was healed at that Bible camp last night! I want to go back again tonight."

Mother said, "I'll go with you."

They were taking pledges at the meeting that night, to pay for the cost of operating the camp. My parents, always faithful givers, handed in a $25 pledge card. When the usher reported that the pledge came from Paynesville, camp leader F. J. Lindquist turned to Ivan O. Miller and asked, "Where's Paynesville? We don't have a church there."

A young minister by the name of O. W. Klingsheim overheard the question and was immediately impressed by the Holy Spirit to start a church in that community. A week later, this young pastor drove to Paynesville, found our farm, and told my father that he wanted to pioneer a church in the Paynesville community. Dad said, "That would be good, but you'd starve here. My family would be the only ones attending."

Brother Klingsheim said, "The Lord called me to do it, so I'm not worried!"

The first Assemblies of God church in Paynesville started with services in our farmhouse. Later, as more and more people came, it was decided to build a church. I still remember the morning my father walked down our driveway behind two Belgian horses, pulling a scraper. He walked three and a half miles into Paynesville, and dug out a hole for a basement church.

Living a Lie

I was impressed with my parents' faith, and the way they put that faith into action. But I was not so impressed with the state of my own faith. Although our little basement church was soon filled with new converts, and although people were being saved and filled with the Spirit and called into the ministry, I was not one of them.

Still, when kids my own age began to stand up during testimony services and say they were glad they were saved, I felt excluded. So I decided to fake it. I, too, stood up one night and testified that I was glad I was a Christian.

It's hard to say the effect that this had. Living a lie is, of course, never easy. I do know that, some years later when I sincerely went forward to pray for salvation, I never could seem to feel that I had connected with God. I went to the altar over and over, even one time going up to my mother at the piano and asking her to pray for my salvation, but nothing seemed to happen within my heart.

Matters were made worse the day that our pastor stopped at the farm to pick up my older brother, Orrin. Orrin was going back to Minneapolis, to continue his studies at North Central for the ministry. As my brother was loading his suitcases into the car, our pastor turned

The Call of God

to me and said, "There's room for you, Arvid. You might just as well come along, too."

I was taken completely by surprise. This was not in my plans! But my mother overheard our conversation, and immediately encouraged me to take advantage of the opportunity.

Like Moses when faced with God's call, I made excuses. "But I haven't packed any clothes—and I don't even have a suitcase!"

Mother pulled out an old suitcase, and hurried to gather some clothes.

"But Dad, I know you need me to help on the farm."

"No, Arvid, you go ahead. We'll get along here."

This was amazing to me. I had not even been able to finish high school, because I was needed on the farm. Much as I had wanted to further my education, it simply was impractical for me to do chores in the morning, walk the six-mile round trip, do more chores, and find time for homework, too. And, of course, extracurricular activities such as football and baseball were out, no matter how much I wanted to play, or how much the coach tried to persuade me to join the teams.

But here I was on my way to college—and Bible college, no less—at the age of sixteen. Small wonder that I was overwhelmed at this sudden turn of events, and troubled about the new and uncharted course I was on.

At the college, Orrin told me to wait in a vacant room while he tried to get the admissions office to let me enroll. Once alone, tears flooded my eyes. I no longer had the security of life back on the farm. I didn't know what was going to happen. And I had no strong sense of God's leading. After all, I had lied about being a Christian; how could I expect it?

When Orrin came back with the good news that the college had a permanent room for us, and would consider enrolling me even though I hadn't graduated from high school, I was still crying quietly. But I stopped, and filled out the application to attend North Central Bible Institute. When I came to the question that asked when and where I was saved, I knew my application wouldn't be accepted if I didn't lie again. I wrote "Years ago in Paynesville".

Move, and I Will Move

Blessed Assurance

I was managing my studies and enjoying college. But one day a revival broke out in chapel. A fellow student stood and admitted publicly that he had been faking that he was a Christian, but now needed the Lord as his Savior, and asked students and faculty to pray for him. Many students gathered around and prayed while he fully surrendered his life to Jesus Christ.

Miller Hall, NCBI, 1930's

Fifteen rows back, I knew I was in a similar condition. I slid to my knees, deeply touched, and tried once again to break through the distance that existed between me and God. I cried out to God to remove the chasm. Then all at once the truth of the Scriptures I had heard all along dawned on me. It wasn't my job to bridge that gap! Suddenly it was as if God himself spoke to me, saying, "My Son, Jesus has already bridged it for you. He has paid the price for your sins. All you need to do is tell Him you fully believe that He is your Savior, and you are my child." For the first time, faith filled my heart, and I began to thank Jesus that He was indeed my Savior.

Suddenly, I experienced such an assurance of salvation that I began to laugh and cry uncontrollably at the same time. I didn't want anyone to notice my strange actions and wonder if I had lost my senses, so I retired to the dorm room I shared with my brother, Orrin. I sat on my bed, still laughing uncontrollably, when my brother walked in and asked what had happened to me.

"Orrin," I said through my tears of joy, "I've just received assurance that I'm truly saved."

'Arvid! That's wonderful!"

The Call of God

Beginning to Serve

With my newfound joy, I wanted to serve. I became active in the department of music, which was led by Rev. Emil Balliet. I joined the orchestra, choir, male chorus, and eventually became a member of the Evangel Male Quartet which traveled through many mid-western states conducting services and doing student procurement work during the summers of 1940 and '41.

We boys in the quartet took turns giving the sermon. So once every four services, I preached. I was beginning to feel that God might truly be calling me to the ministry. But I did not think I wanted to do evangelistic work. I was a farmer by upbringing; I liked not only to plant the seed, but also to tend it, and share in the harvest. I thought it would be wonderful to start a church, and help it to grow.

Baptized in the Spirit

One day while attending classes in my senior year, our instructor, Rev. F. J. Lindquist, was late to class. While we were waiting, someone suggested that the class could spend the time praying, so we knelt and began to pray.

After awhile most of the class got back on their seats, but four of us guys continued praying. Finally Rev. Lindquist arrived, sized up the situation and suggested the class should proceed with studies, and if there were those who wanted to continue praying, they should excuse themselves and go to a prayer room.

Well, we just got up and left the room and found a small prayer room on the fourth floor, and it was there that I was gloriously filled with the Holy Spirit.

Finally the time came when I had to go to my job as an elevator operator. I was so full of the joy of the Lord, I was still speaking in tongues as I moved students from floor to floor in North Central's five story building.

So How *Did* God Call You, Arvid?

That cold winter's day in 1941, as I sat on the hard folding chair and reviewed the events that had brought me to this place, I found I could

Move, and I Will Move

not answer the presbyters' question with one single experience. I had seen no burning bush. I had heard no audible voice. I had no dramatic and unmistakable experience to point to, that would impress the men sitting around the table in Miller Hall.

But what I did have was a steady and persistent tug on my life. A sense that God had the reins, and He was steering me in a certain direction—a direction that had been set at the tender age of nine, when I first sensed God's majesty and power.

God had called me then, though I was not fully aware of all it would mean.

God called me, too, through the faith of my parents, through daily devotions and their acts of courage and sacrifice, through a miraculous healing.

God kept His hand on me through my lies, and my pretending that all was well, and my foolish attempts to try to get to Him by my own strength.

God showed up in circumstance: a pastor tossing off an invitation, a mother who packed my suitcase, a father who put a harvest of souls ahead of a harvest of grain, a college that admitted an untutored boy.

God called to me through scripture, through a classmate's confession, direct to my heart while I was on my knees.

He baptized me with His Holy Spirit in a flood of joy, and inspired me to join college musical groups that spread the gospel, in which I was given the opportunity to speak from a pulpit.

What else could I do but preach the gospel? All of God's gentle tugs on the reins had led me inescapably to this hard chair and a board of faithful presbyters, men of God who searched my face and searched my heart. I had no doubt that I had been called.

The doubt in my heart was this: could I measure up?

2
Measuring Up

"Be diligent to present yourself approved to God, a worker who does not need to be ashamed, rightly dividing the word of truth."
2 Timothy 2:15

I always wanted to see how I measured up against everyone else. Why that was, I'm not sure.

Maybe it had something to do with a fear of failure. On the farm, I lived through a three year drought and the Great Depression; the threat of failure hung over our heads at all times.

Maybe it had something to do with my father. My dad put a lot of confidence in me, and I had a longing to live up to that, to do well and deserve his good opinion.

It probably had a lot to do with the fact that I didn't get past the ninth grade. It was deeply wounding to me that I was unable to continue my education. The year that I should have been in tenth grade, I was needed on the farm. I remember that a feeling of desperation came over me as I looked out at the endless fields, and I thought, "I'll never get out of here."

When at last I had the chance to go to college, I felt a burning desire to prove that I was just as smart and capable as everyone else. I was anxious to discover how I measured up against them mentally, in the classroom, and physically, on the playing field.

But there was another measure that I learned how to use at North

Move, and I Will Move

Central, and that was a measure of the spirit. Measuring myself against God's yardstick always left me humble, and intensely aware of my need for help.

And help did come to me, in the shape of exceptional teachers. Six of my instructors in particular stand out as I recall my growth during those formative college years.

Measuring Up Mentally

Anna Froland, Etiquette

Anna Froland was tall and soft-spoken, with a graceful manner. She taught us proper etiquette, painting word pictures to show us how to conduct ourselves in a wide variety of social situations. She helped change an awkward, clumsy, uneducated farmer boy into a young minister who could meet with people in many different circumstances, from all different walks of life, with courtesy and confidence. How grateful I was for this.

She always assumed the best of everyone, probably because she was so genuinely good herself! She took such an interest in people that everyone loved her. I've always remembered her teaching and good example.

Gladys Balliet, Typing

This small, slender woman taught me typing one summer. She would walk up and down the aisles, giving us pointers. When something tickled her, she had such an infectious laugh that it made me want to laugh right along with her.

I made plenty of mistakes at first, so I had a lot to laugh about. But she was so kind and patient with me that I worked ever so hard to become proficient.

At the time, I had no idea how much I would use the skill, but it was very useful to me all throughout my ministry. Even in my retirement, I am at the keyboard several hours a day. I can still hear her voice, saying "My, Arvid, you're doing so well."

Emil Balliet, Music

Emil Balliet was director of music and husband of Gladys Balliet, and had a good sense of humor just like his wife. He had dark, curly hair, a strong baritone voice, and played the violin. He seemed to do everything well—which was a good thing, as he had to direct the choir, the male chorus, and the orchestra too.

He had a hand in choosing me to be part of the male quartet that traveled in the summer, representing the school, and he taught me phrasing, enunciation, and performance techniques. These skills gave me confidence, which helped me when I played my trombone in churches, camps, and at district and general council meetings.

A. G. Ward, Bible

A. G. Ward was a gentleman of the old school. I never saw him without a jacket and tie. In fact, he told us that a true gentleman is always fully dressed, and that even when he relaxed at home with his wife, he wore—a coat and tie!

He was an earnest, intense, very conscientious man. Life was a serious business to him, and most serious of all was the study of the word of God. When, in my freshman year, I got a poor grade on one of his Bible exams, he called me into his office.

"Arvid," he said, "please sit down." And then, to my astonishment, he began to cry! Through his tears, he gave the correct answers to the questions I had missed, saying, "Arvid, I know you can do better than this. I want to pray for you, that you will work at applying yourself."

A.G. Ward

I might have thought this to be overly dramatic, had it been anyone else. But when I was in the presence of this man, I felt the presence of the Lord.

Suddenly I found tears in my own eyes as well. It moved me that a man of his stature would take such a personal interest in how I turned out as a minister of the gospel.

A. G. Ward influenced me in ways that no other instructor did, and from that moment on, I began to take a new interest in my preparation for the ministry.

Move, and I Will Move

C. M. Ward, Prophecy, Expository Preaching

This man was A. G. Ward's son, but he was not so serious.

C. M. Ward was a rotund man who loved to eat and loved to preach. He said that he got his exercise, walking back and forth on the platform. Deliberate and self-assured, he had an authoritative voice that made people want to listen; he commanded respect from everyone the moment he walked into the room.

He taught prophecy—Revelation as well as the major and minor prophets—and told us we should not preach from the book of Revelation until we'd been in ministry at least twenty years! He opened the scriptures to me in a way I'll never forget.

He taught expository preaching, too, and was in great demand as a speaker. He was gone nearly every weekend, preaching in one of our churches in Minnesota or a neighboring state. Occasionally, he would invite me along to play my trombone at the services.

One day I stepped into his office and noticed newspaper clippings scattered all over his desk. He explained that was the way he kept abreast of current happenings in the world. It showed me why he was becoming such an interesting preacher, and inspired me to widen my world and take a greater interest in current events.

President Frank J. Lindquist, Doctrine

Frank J. Lindquist was a leader wherever he went. He was my doctrine teacher, and he made the inspired word of God come alive to us students. I respected his wise and sound teaching so much that on Sundays, I would walk two and a half miles from North Central to the Minneapolis Gospel Tabernacle at 13th and Lake Street, just to hear him again. He was pastor there, and the church was always packed with people.

He was about six feet tall, with a strong voice that stood out in a crowd. He was a man of great faith who had pioneered many churches in Minnesota (with James D. Menzie, later my father-in-law). He also started the Minneapolis Gospel Tabernacle[1], Lake Geneva Bible Camp[2], and North Central Bible Institute[3] for the training of young

---

[1] Later renamed Christ's Church
[2] Later renamed Lake Geneva Christian Center
[3] Later renamed North Central Bible College, now known as North Central University

people for ministry at home and abroad. He kept all three going through the Great Depression, which is a testament both to his leadership and to God's hand on his work.

In its over seven decades of existence, North Central has helped train thousands of young people who have obeyed the call of God and gone on to preach the Gospel all over the world! Daniel 12:3 talks about F. J. Lindquist's eternal reward: *"Those who are wise shall shine like the brightness of the firmament; and those who turn many to righteousness like the stars forever and ever."*

Near the end of his life, I visited Brother Lindquist every week. And each time I came, he was just full of the joy of the Lord. Even as he lay dying, he was still so happy! It was a great encouragement to me. He was still my teacher, even in his last moments on earth.

Executive V. P. Ivan O. Miller, Pastoral Theology

Ivan O. Miller was not as strongly built as F. J. Lindquist, but he had a gaze of such intensity that it seemed to pierce right though me. When I saw him looking at me, I would have the involuntary reaction— "What did I do wrong?" But he was very kind to me.

Ivan O. Miller loved the word of God, and made us want to love it too. His teaching filled me with a sense of awe about becoming a pastor. He had a passion for pioneering churches, and tried to inspire us toward that end.

I remember sitting in class when he said, "We need people to go out and start churches!" Something inside me responded strongly to that. I began to feel that starting a church, and helping it grow, was the direction I should be headed. And once I had graduated, Brother Miller was one of the voices encouraging me to start a church in Little Falls—and later still, in Bloomington.

Measuring Up Physically
A Little Belt Tightening

As a student, I was poor. Ivan O. Miller knew this, and kindly gave me jobs where I could earn the money I needed for books and tuition, including one at the school laundry, where I supervised a number of women who worked the washing machines and wringers. I liked that job much better than dishwashing (I did that only one day and never went back), or picking up dead bodies for the local mortuary (an awkward task, especially going down stairs).

So I was not a student who had extra money to spend. I was used to this; having just gone through a three year drought on the farm amid the Great Depression, I was no stranger to a little belt-tightening. But having a room that was just across the hall from the confectionery was practically cruel and unusual punishment.

Working in the NCBI laundry.

Night after night, I would listen to the chatter of students across the hall, and smell the tantalizing aroma of hamburgers, or ice cream, or popcorn as it drifted through the transom into my dorm. I so wanted to join them, as I was always hungry, but I didn't have any money; so I just sat in my room and suffered.

One night I told a classmate who was visiting me that I was so hungry, I could eat an entire pint of ice cream. He wouldn't believe it, and said he'd put up the money for a pint, just to prove me wrong. I took him up on the offer in a hurry, and you guessed it—I ate the whole thing. It tasted soooo good!

I discovered that when something good happened to me, as it did that night, it gave me a lot of optimism for the future. Keeping my stomach happy wasn't very spiritual, perhaps, but I discovered that taking care of my body was a good way to improve my attitude.

Playing Ball

All my life, I loved sports. On the farm, we played ball after chores— and if it was Sunday, Dad would say, "Just go over the hill, so the neighbors don't see." He knew, unlike some who were stricter, that

Measuring Up

the Sabbath was made for man, not man for the Sabbath—and that refreshment of the body through sports was important for any growing boy.

In high school, I did not play after-school sports, for I was needed on the farm. But I loved anything having to do with a ball, and I had a hankering to measure myself against others. In college, we often played football or baseball in the park, and I gained in confidence as I saw I could not only hold my own, but could compete well. I never felt the need to argue with the referee, because I began to feel that, whether the call went against me or not, I could always play well enough to make it up.

One day, word got around that the great Morris Williams, a young man who was known as a star in North Dakota for his prowess in six man football, was coming to North Central. I felt an inner surge of interest, and a keen sense of wanting to test myself against him.

So when we played football, I got a big kick out of tackling him. Once, my brother Orrin and I both tackled him together—one high, one low—and Morris had to speak as a Christian athlete at a service the next day. I'm afraid I have to admit that he went to the platform on crutches! (Morris William's twin sister, Dorris, later married my brother Harland.)

This love of sports was a strength in my life, though I didn't realize it then. Because I was so motivated to hit a ball, any ball, I was kept active, and healthy.

And I found that physical activity was a way to keep things in perspective. Situations that were bothering me always looked better after a hard played game, and taking time out for physical recreation helped keep me from burnout—an occupational hazard for anyone in ministry.

That's Mind and Body—
But What About the Spirit?

I was measuring up well in the classroom and on the playing field. But I was painfully aware of my need for spiritual growth.

God graciously granted me the assurance of salvation that I needed—and gloriously filled me with the Holy Spirit. These personal experiences with God were very precious to me. But I knew I needed more.

A life of faith—a growing, vibrant spiritual life—is more than an inner experience. It must involve action. It should affect people and events in the real world.

It requires learning to pray.

3
Learning To Pray

"...Not lagging in diligence, fervent in spirit, serving the Lord; rejoicing in hope, patient in tribulation, continuing steadfastly in prayer..."

Romans 12:11-12

So how does one grow spiritually? Romans 5:3-5 gives a step by step approach.

Trials and testing bring about perseverance. Perseverance results in proven character. Proven character brings hope—and, according to Paul, hope does not disappoint, because our hope is in God whose love has been poured out in our hearts through the Holy Spirit.

But if trials and testing bring about perseverance, how does it happen? Is it just a matter of grimly hanging on until the trouble ends?

I think there is more to it than that. God wants us to meet the trials actively with prayer. As we go to our knees in utter dependence, He grows our faith.

Paul himself makes the connection further on, in Romans 12:12. After telling Christians they should fervently serve the Lord, and rejoice in hope, he adds this: *"...patient in tribulation, continuing steadfastly in prayer."*

I learned to pray at North Central—and, as you might expect, my prayer life grew as I was faced with trouble.

Move, and I Will Move

Crisis Prayers
North Central Needs a Miracle

I was sitting in chapel one day in 1938, when Ivan O. Miller, our executive vice president, stepped to the podium to speak to the student body.

"We're having great difficulty paying our bills," he said. "Unless there is a miracle, our electric power will be shut off."

A sudden feeling of foreboding filled the chapel, as Rev. Miller went on to tell us that many other accounts remained unpaid as well.

But our leaders knew where to go for help. They called a solemn assembly, and we were all asked to humble ourselves before the Lord in prayer and fasting. We did so, imploring God to perform a miracle so that the school wouldn't have to close its doors.

Ivan O. Miller

The news that North Central was having problems paying its bills reached a potato farmer in southern Minnesota, and so he offered to give a truckload of his potatoes if people from the school would come down and pick them up.

Here was something I could do! I volunteered to help.

We found someone with a big truck, and off we went to fill the truck with newly harvested potatoes. There were four of us, though, and there was only room for three in the cab.

I offered to ride on top of the load of potatoes for the 150 mile trip back to North Central. That turned out to be one of the coldest rides I've ever had, but we all felt good that we could help North Central in a small way.

Trouble + Prayer = Revival

A. G. Ward, the Bible teacher who had wept over my poor exam, became very ill and was not expected to live. The students and faculty prayed earnestly for his healing.

One day he sent word that God had given him a promise. He had been reading the story of Hezekiah in 2 Kings 20, which says:

> *In those days Hezekiah was sick and near death. And Isaiah the prophet... went to him and said to him, "Thus says the Lord, 'Set your house in order, for you shall die, and not live.' " Then he turned his face toward the wall and prayed to the Lord... Then it happened, before Isaiah had gone out into the middle court, that the word of the Lord came to him saying, 'Return and tell Hezekiah... I have heard your prayer, I have seen your tears; surely I will heal you... and I will add to your days fifteen years.'*

A. G. Ward asked God to do the same for him, and felt that he had been given that promise. He not only recovered, but true to the word God had given him, he lived to have fifteen more years of ministry.

This turn of events lifted the faith of everyone who heard of it. The student body began to earnestly seek the Lord. As a result, the financial picture began to improve.

Something else happened as a result of all this prayer. Revival came to North Central. Classes were dismissed for several days as God moved powerfully among us. Many students were baptized in the Spirit, and some received calls to missionary work. And for weeks thereafter, North Central experienced a deep and continuous seeking of the face of God.

How Can I Pray When I'm Half Asleep?

Although we earnestly prayed in times of trouble, North Central placed great emphasis on prayer at all times. The subject of prayer was often highlighted by faculty members in the chapel services when they spoke, and also in the classrooms. The entire student body was organized into what were called Mission Prayer Bands, in which we prayed for the mission field of our choice.

The school set up twenty-four hour prayer chains, and students signed up for a specific time of day. We had to sign in and out, so our leaders could know if we kept our commitment. The hour I chose was from 1:00 – 2:00 a.m.

That was the longest hour of my day! I'd pray awhile, then look at my watch, and pray some more. Many times, I'd wake up from an accidental nap, and try to begin again.

I needed help—and I found it in the library. *Power Through Prayer* by E.M. Bounds and a book on the life of John "Praying" Hyde were a great blessing to me.

After graduation, there were no students reminding me to pray, no faculty members preaching inspiring messages on the subject of prayer. I found that I was all alone, and that presented a different challenge.

One day I was listening to the leader of a men's Bible study list a number of prayer requests. When he asked for additional requests, I said, "I do my best praying when I'm in trouble. So you could help my prayer life, by praying that I have troubles!"

The fellows all laughed at that because it was such an unusual request, but there was a lot of truth to it.

I Cry Out to God

Troubles do tend to turn us to God for help, and if this happens, it can be a blessing in disguise. I've done some of my most effective praying when I was facing problems which were beyond my ability to solve.

After graduation in the spring of 1941, I went on a summer-long ministry tour with the Evangel quartet. When I returned to North Central in the fall, someone asked me, "How is your brother Orrin?"

"Is there something wrong?" I asked quickly. "I haven't heard a thing because I've been on the road, traveling."

There was a heavy pause. Finally I was told that my beloved brother had been stricken with spinal meningitis, and was not expected to live.

A quick call home confirmed it. Orrin was in terrible pain, and near death. Mother said, "Pray, Arvid!" I felt a surge of compassion overwhelm me. I ran down to the school basement where the furnaces were, and in this hidden place began to cry out to God to save my brother's life.

Orrin was special to me. I couldn't accept the doctor's diagnosis that he was about to die. I continued praying in the Spirit 'with groanings which cannot be uttered'[4] for quite some time, until at last I felt the burden lift from my heart.

[4] Romans 8:26 (KJV).

The next morning I called home and heard the news.

Orrin had been curled up tightly in a fetal position. Even the slightest sound—a car passing on the road, for example—caused him to cringe in torment. But suddenly, at 3:00 a.m., he relaxed and fell asleep. The doctor was astounded.

At 7:00 a.m. Orrin woke up, hungry. He was so weak still that my mother had to feed him with an eyedropper. But within days he was walking—a very quick recovery for that type of illness. You can imagine the praise that went up from all of us who loved him!

I'm not saying that my brother was healed when I prayed, because there were many others who prayed as well. But I'm convinced that Orrin's illness turned out to be a blessing in disguise for him, for me, our entire family, and many others.

Orrin had a call on his life to preach the gospel, but after this experience, his ministry emphasis was praying for the sick. God used him powerfully, and many divine healings took place under his ministry after that.

But Why Wait for Trouble?

At North Central, there was a room designated for committee meetings that was seldom used. One day, I decided to go there just because I felt I needed to spend a little time praying.

As I prepared to pray, I realized that I had no special prayer request. I wasn't even facing any particular assignment or forthcoming responsibility—and I knew that I did my best praying when I had some urgent need!

So I asked the Lord to teach me. I asked Him to show me how to be faithful to meet with Him on a regular basis, even when there was no crisis or trouble to face.

And the Lord spoke to my heart, saying, "You need me now, and you will always need me in the now!"

The truth of this dawned on me. All of my future moments: minutes, hours, days, weeks, months and years still to come, will some time be 'right now' for me. But God experiences all times in the now.

I'd fallen into the habit of using prayer to help me escape from trouble, or to help me measure up, to perform well through assignments I'd been given. But the Lord was teaching me that He wanted me close to Him all the time.

So I prayed, "Lord, I need you always. Please help me treat every future moment like I've been treating those special assignment or crisis moments." Suddenly, I felt I needed God's presence—now.

The apostle Paul wrote in 2 Corinthians 6:2, *"Behold, NOW is the accepted time; behold, NOW is the day of salvation."* That implies that God, our Father who is always living in the now, is ever ready to share His salvation, His presence, and His power with me—right now.

I'm a father myself. And while I love to help my children whenever I can, still our relationship would suffer if they only talked to me when they wanted something!

My connection with my children becomes more meaningful when they let me in on the ordinary things, the funny things, the daily happenings of their lives. And even if we're not saying much of anything, it is wonderful just to be in the same room, aware of their life and presence and what they mean to me.

In the same way, my relationship with the Lord has become much more meaningful since I've been practicing an awareness of His presence in my life, moment by moment. That day in the prayer room, God simply and tenderly let me know that He wanted me to love Him for who He was, not just for what He could do for me.

And Now I Really Start Praying!

I thought I had really learned to pray at North Central. But in the summer following my graduation, I met a girl.

Her name was Marian. She was just fifteen. And once I met her, my prayers took on a new urgency.

"Lord," I prayed, "is this the one?"

Some of my friends said an emphatic "No!"

How could I know for sure? How does God guide us in the choice of a mate?

4

When You Make Up Your Mind, Let Me Know

"For you shall go out with joy, and be led out with peace..."
Isaiah 55:12a

"Don't marry her, Arvid. She'll ruin your ministry."

The speaker, a man I considered my friend, shook his head as he pronounced this verdict. I was dumbfounded.

I had been holding meetings with a faculty member and two friends from North Central, when one of them took me aside. Apparently they had all discussed my engagement to Marian Menzie on the long ride to Little Falls, and the verdict was unanimous. Marian was not the right girl for me.

What was I supposed to say to that?

I tried to be courteous. I thanked him—and then I promptly ignored his warning.

I knew better.

And after sixty years of happy marriage, I guess you could say I've been proven right.

But how could I know then? How does God guide us in the choice of a life's partner?

Perhaps the best way to explain is just to tell our stories.

Move, and I Will Move

Arvid: I had not really dated in college, unless you count sitting by a particular girl in church. I guess I kept myself a bit aloof, socially. I had friends who would spend hours socializing in the halls of North Central, in the evening, and I remember thinking, 'What a waste of time. There's so much else they could be doing!'

But the summer following my graduation, when I was doing a last tour with the male quartet, we made a stop at a church in Gary, Indiana. And as I sat

Evangel Quartet, 1941. Arvid Kingsriter on the far right, Jimmy Nicholson on the far left.

on the platform before the evening service was to begin, I noticed a beautiful blond girl sitting in the auditorium.

When the song leader came to the platform, he called this young lady to come play the piano. As she approached, I whispered to Jimmy Nicholson, our quartet leader, "Who's *that*?"

"That's Pastor Menzie's daughter!"

Well, right away I started scheming. I had to get to know her better! And as I listened to her skillful accompaniment on the piano, I was even more impressed. Suddenly, spending time socializing didn't seem like a waste at all.

After the service, I checked to see where I was supposed to stay that night. Sure enough, Pastor Menzie was hosting two of us—but I had been assigned to the other home.

That didn't stop me for long. I pulled the strings I had to pull in order to get our leader to reassign me.

And that night, I went to the home of Rev. James D. Menzie—a respected pastor, a man who had pioneered churches in Minnesota with Frank J. Lindquist—and the father of a girl I couldn't stop thinking about.

When You Make Up Your Mind, Let Me Know

Marian: At fifteen, I wasn't thinking of marriage at all. I was just hoping that my parents would let me date sometime before the millennium.

Besides, I had a very low opinion of Bible colleges. And I certainly wasn't interested in marrying any man who was planning to become a minister.

It was hard enough, I thought, being a pastor's daughter. The last thing I wanted was to become some preacher's wife.

But I was a teenage girl, and so of course when four new young men came to our church one night, I looked them over. "Well," I thought to myself, "they're from that *Bible* college... but if I had to pick one, which one would I choose?" And I picked Arvid.

At that moment, I seemed to hear in my head, "You're going to marry him."

I chuckled to myself—but instantly a scripture from the second chapter of Luke came to my mind: *"But Mary kept all these things, and pondered them in her heart."*

Was it God who was speaking to me? I felt it was, but then I was only fifteen. I hadn't had a lot of experience with hearing the voice of God.

Besides, the young man in question was a Bible student, planning to become a pastor—exactly the type of person I wanted most to avoid.

"Well," I thought skeptically, "we'll see."

I decided that if this was of God, then it would happen without my doing anything at all. So I didn't do any of the usual things a girl might do when she was making a play for a boy. I didn't laugh, or try to talk to him, or even look at him—I just ignored him.

But then he came to my house.

Arvid: Ever since I was a boy, I'd prayed earnestly for my future wife. I'd tell the Lord that I was sure my wife-to-be was living now, and I prayed for her parents too, to have the wisdom to bring her up well.

I'd never seen anyone yet who'd impressed me the way Marian did.

Her mother was out of town at the time, so the responsibility fell on her to take care of the household and the extra guests.

She cooked for us; and she was a good cook. She was wearing a dress that she'd sewn; and it looked wonderful on her. I watched the way she went about doing things, and I liked everything she did. And I had already heard her play the piano and sing.

Marian Menzie, age 15.

You know, it seemed the decision had already been made. I felt a real clarity about it from the very beginning. Once I met Marian, there was no one else who even appealed to me—all that remained was the process of waiting for her to grow up.

Of course, I didn't know how Marian felt.

Marian: Arvid asked me to write to him.

But I had seen him with his friends, and one of the boys had been passing around a letter that a girl had written, so I said "No." I wasn't interested in writing letters that might get passed around and laughed at!

But when Arvid promised that he would never show my letters to anyone, I believed him. And so we started to correspond.

When I went to school, grade skipping was common. If you were quick at your studies, you'd be advanced by half a grade at a time. So the summer I was fifteen, I only had one more year of high school left.

I was mature for my age—physically, anyway—and felt more than ready to go to college. I planned to go to Wheaton. It was a Christian college with a fine reputation; and instead of dances, which I wasn't allowed to attend, they had many elegant formal events.

That summer before college, though, I went to Lake Geneva Bible Camp, where my father was speaking.

Arvid: The summer of 1942, I was assistant pastor at a church in Iowa, but I wanted to get to camp to see Marian. I hitchhiked from Sioux City to Alexandria, Minnesota, and then I promptly borrowed my brother Harland's car. I wanted to take Marian out on the town!

After dinner, and an ice cream soda, we came back to the camp and took a little walk. It was a romantic, moonlit summer's night, and she was so beautiful. I kissed her.

And then I held her hand, and asked if we could pray together about the future of our relationship. And so we did.

Marian: I was so looking forward to Wheaton. I'd even gotten a little evening bag for the formals... but something in me was unsettled. I began to feel more and more strongly that I was not supposed to go to Wheaton—that God had something else in mind.

Oh, I fought against it. It was not what I wanted. But at last, sure in my spirit that I would have no peace if I went against God's plan, I applied to North Central Bible Institute. Imagine! Me, going to Bible school! And Arvid wasn't even there, to make things interesting.

I dated other boys at school. But wouldn't you know it, Arvid kept showing up... and if he came into town, I cancelled everything. By the time I was eighteen, we were engaged to be married—*against* the advice of his friends.

Arvid: Three of my friends very seriously warned me not to marry Marian. She was too worldly, they said. She liked wearing lipstick and heels, and she wore sweaters and pearls... too young, too flighty, too vain, they said. She wouldn't make a good pastor's wife, they said.

I listened, and quietly disagreed, and then forgot about it. I knew she was the one for me.

How could I know?

I'm not sure. I just never had any doubt. And when God gives a clarity of vision like that, it's best not to turn your back on it.

Marian: I didn't know at the time that Arvid's friends had cautioned him not to marry me. He kept that information to himself for years. But if I had known, I can't imagine that I would have taken their warnings very seriously. I loved Arvid, and I knew myself.

I wasn't perfect, but I didn't think a pastor's wife had to make herself plain, or stop having fun, in order to look like someone else's idea of holy.

But shortly before our wedding, I heard of three couples—Christian couples, whose weddings I had attended in the past year—whose marriages were floundering. And it frightened me.

I was so naïve. I was only nineteen, and had grown up reading Grace Livingston Hill books, where Christian boy meets Christian girl, and everyone lives happily ever after. I guess I thought that if you married a Christian, what could go wrong?

Suddenly I had a serious case of cold feet.

Arvid, who had been pioneering a church in Little Falls, had driven down for one last date before our wedding. I broke the news to him as we talked in the car— "I'm not sure I want to get married."

He let go my hand, started up the car, and said, "Well, when you make up your mind, let me know."

Arvid: There wasn't anything else to say. I figured that about covered it. But inside, I was shocked.

Was I really going to lose the life's mate that God had brought into my life? And what would our friends and relatives think?

The wedding invitations had already been sent. The church had been booked. Not only that, but her father had even agreed to be the commencement speaker for Marian's graduation from North Central, since he was coming to Minneapolis anyway to conduct our wedding!

We had made other commitments, too. Two pastors in California, Robert Renfroe and Don Weston, had each been kind enough to schedule two-week revival meetings with us. I was to speak, and Marian was to play the piano, and the pastors had already distributed advertising among their churches. Marian and I had been thrilled at the way everything had miraculously fallen into place. And now she was questioning?

I was not only shocked—I was angry.

On the hundred mile drive back to Little Falls, I talked to God very earnestly. I said, "God, there's no reason this wedding needs to be cancelled. We've not only made these commitments, but You are the one who's helped us to make them. You brought us together, You kept us together for four years, and You prepared us for marriage... You just have to speak to Marian. Just please give her Your assurance that our marriage will be happy and successful."

By the time I arrived back at the apartment in Little Falls, God had given me the assurance that He had not only brought us together, but He would continue his work in and through us.

You know, I didn't know how God would answer. But I remembered this scripture: *"Great peace have they which love Thy law, and nothing shall offend them."*[5]

I went to bed and slept like a baby. And the next day, I went about my pastoral duties with a heart filled with God's peace.

Marian: I went to class at North Central the next day, very troubled.

It was May. I was almost ready to graduate. My mother had been planning my wedding, and the preparations were virtually complete.

But it had finally registered that getting married wasn't just starry eyes and a handsome groom. It hit me—marriage was for the rest of my life! How could I possibly know if it was right for me to marry Arvid?

Well—I prayed. And I'm not recommending this method now, but I think God sees us in our simple faith and answers us accordingly. I sat in the back of that classroom, totally ignoring the professor, and I said to God, "I'm going to open my Bible and put my finger down, and I want you to give me a verse that will tell me what to do."

So I opened my Bible, and my finger landed on a passage of scripture in Isaiah 55, and most specifically on verse eleven: *"So shall my word be that goes forth from my mouth; it shall not return to me void, but it shall accomplish what I please, and it shall prosper in the thing for which I sent it."*

Immediately I recalled the moment when I had first seen Arvid, and the voice that had spoken to my heart—that he was the man who would become my husband. I felt that God was speaking to me again, saying, "That word in your heart? That was from me. And I'm not taking it back."

I felt a sudden confidence that God would accomplish His will—our marriage—and that with His help, our marriage would succeed.

With an overflowing heart, I went on to read verses 12 and 13: *"For you shall go out with joy, and be led out with peace; the mountains and the hills shall break forth into singing before you, and all the trees of the field shall clap their hands. Instead of the thorn shall come up the cypress tree; and instead*

---

[5] Psalm 119:165. (KJV)

of the brier shall come up the myrtle tree; and it shall be to the Lord for a name, for an everlasting sign that shall not be cut off."

I called Arvid as soon as class was dismissed. "God has given me the assurance I needed," I told him. "Thank you for being patient with me. I'm ready to marry you on May 19."

Arvid: At this writing, we are planning our 60th wedding anniversary. To God be all the glory!

I would like to quote from a valentine that Marian gave me recently:

"For the one I love. After so many years of picking out valentines for you, I feel like I've already said 'I love you' in every way possible. But I don't know if I've put into words how grateful I am that we've come through so much together or how sharing my life with you means even more to me as time goes by.

I only hope you know that after so many years, I love you in so many ways. I never cease to be amazed that at our young ages, only fifteen and nineteen, we found each other. Surely, God let our paths cross–our eyes meet–our hearts given and our lives forever joined.

And ever since, I have been so proud to stand beside you–proud of who you are and what you have accomplished. You have lived at home what you have preached in the pulpit. Not all wives have been so fortunate.

As we march day by day to the end of this partnership, I cherish every hour in every day.

Love, Marian"

Marian: Even today, after 59 years of marriage, I am moved to tears when I think of how God spoke to me as a naïve nineteen year old girl, on the verge of either her life's great partnership—or her life's great regret.

How could I possibly know? I couldn't. But God knew. And He was faithful, and is faithful, and will be faithful, to witness to our hearts through His Spirit and His word.

5

Starting at the Bottom

"Your ears shall hear a word behind you, saying, 'This is the way, walk in it,' whenever you turn to the right hand or whenever you turn to the left."

Isaiah 30:21

Three ladies in overcoats and galoshes sat on a hard plank bench one Sunday night, huddled close to an oil drum stove. Behind them were row after row of empty benches—enough to seat 500—and before them was their young, inexperienced pastor, picking out a chorus on the piano with one finger.

It was December of 1942. I had just turned twenty-one, and this was my first church.

Technically, I suppose it was my second. I had, after all, served for a year as assistant pastor at a church in Sioux City, Iowa. But this was a pioneering effort, and for the first time I was entirely on my own. This tiny congregation was all I had to show for two weeks of special meetings in Little Falls, Minnesota, and several more weeks of visiting and preaching.

The temperature in the uninsulated building was dropping rapidly, and I had a dilemma. How could I keep the service going, and still add wood to the stoves? I decided to start another song, and tell the ladies to keep singing. I thought I could fill the stoves and get back before the song ended, if I ran.

Move, and I Will Move

The stoves were crudely made of two oil drums, one on top of the other, with a door at the bottom for wood, and a pipe at the top for a chimney. No safety inspector today would allow them, especially in a wooden building with a sawdust floor! But we had four, and on this frosty winter's night they grew so hot that the metal became almost transparent. I could see the shape of the wood right through the steel barrel.

My plan for keeping the service going worked, but at a price. By the time I got back to the piano, the ladies had dropped into another key. And although evangelist R. D. E. Smith had taught me how to accompany choruses with a few basic chords, he had never prepared me for this! I fumbled around on the piano, trying to find notes that matched what the ladies were singing, with no success.

Those painful moments at the piano almost seemed a metaphor for what was happening in my ministry. I was trying hard, but was my ministry successful? I couldn't imagine that anyone would think so.

To make matters worse, a short time before I had visited North Central Bible Institute for an alumni function. A former classmate had run up, thrown his arms around me, and said, "Praise the Lord, Arvid! We don't have to start at the bottom. We can go right to the top!" He went on to tell me about the large and thriving church where he had just been elected pastor. I thought of my three ladies and our leased auditorium, and kept quiet.

How had I gotten to this place—and was I really where God wanted me to be? It was a question I asked myself many times that winter. But each time I wrestled with doubt, I emerged with even more confidence. Yes, I was exactly where God wanted me to be. And with that assurance, I felt that everything was all right, no matter how the circumstances looked to others.

How could I have such confidence that I knew the will of God? How do any of us know, truly, how to discern between what God wants of us, and what is the prompting of our own will?

Sometimes we have a burning bush experience. Sometimes the direction is very clear. But usually it is a process requiring prayer, a search of the scriptures, counsel with trusted advisors, our own good judgment, a heart open toward God—and for me, long walks in the woods.

Starting at the Bottom

Looking Back: How Had I Gotten Here?

The summer of 1941 had been an eventful one. After graduation, and shortly after I'd met Marian, I received letters offering me the position of assistant pastor from two well-known pastors.

The first came from Rev. J. Robert Ashcroft (father of our former attorney general, John Ashcroft) asking me to join his pastoral staff in Chicago, Illinois. The second letter came from Rev. David Hastie, pastor of the Myrtle Street Assemblies of God church in Sioux City, Iowa.

Ashcroft's letter promised a weekly salary of $35. Hastie could promise only room and board in the parsonage—with no salary at all. Which one to accept? Both pastors were respected men of God. Why not simply be sensible and accept the one from the larger church, the job that paid more?

Making the Sensible Decision

It seems logical to make a decision by considering the pros and cons. After giving due weight to each, the most sensible answer often becomes clear.

But for a follower of Christ, the only sensible decision is the one that is God's will. Sometimes, on the surface, that decision can seem less than the best, or even completely foolish. But it really doesn't matter. If we truly believe that God is all knowing, all powerful and all loving, then of course His plans for us are perfect. It only remains for us to discover the next step, and take it.

As I considered the two job offers, I set a pattern for decision-making that has served me my whole life.

When I make a decision, I make it in the fear of God. Let's say I have several options. I'll pray over each one, carefully consider all aspects, and ask God for guidance. After seeking the Lord for a protracted period of time, all of a sudden, something comes alive in me; I sense something, some excitement or spark as I pray about one of the options. That is the Holy Spirit leading me in that direction.

I choose that option, and I don't look back. There's no need to bother with second guessing later, if I make the initial decision in this manner.

Move, and I Will Move

In the summer of 1941, as I took long walks in the woods and prayed about which offer I should accept, I felt more and more impressed to accept the opportunity in Sioux City.

And What Followed the Sensible Decision

In the fall of 1941 I went to Sioux City, Iowa, to live with Rev. and Mrs. David Hastie and their twin boys, Ronald and Roland. I was just nineteen, but I was responsible for the youth program (over 100 in high school and college), directing the choir, and leading the singing in church services. After six months, I was given a salary—a weekly check for $7.50! Believe it or not, I bought government bonds with that money.

I was learning a great deal from Brother Hastie, and I enjoyed my responsibilities, but there was one young man named Jay who was giving me some trouble in the youth group and choir.

He was a leader among the kids,

Arvid Kingsriter, age 19.

and he was having fun being obnoxious. When the young people were gathering, he'd be at the front door, mocking what was happening in the services; and kids would stop and listen.

I don't honestly know if he meant all he said, but it fed his ego to have an audience, so he just kept on. He most likely knew better and felt guilty, but all the same what he was doing was subverting the work of the Holy Spirit among the young people.

I was deeply concerned, but I did not confront Jay. Instead, I spent a good bit of the night in intercessory prayer for him.

Not too long after that, at the close of a service, Jay came to the altar. I had the privilege of praying with him as he consecrated his life to the Lord. And after that, Jay didn't give me any trouble at all.

You know, the Spirit of the Lord just broke that subversive tendency in him; I never had to say a word. And that's the best way.

I always felt, if I saw someone doing a wrong action, that if I confronted him, I might be driving him away and I might never have another opportunity to minister to him.

I was rehearsing the choir on the afternoon of December 7, 1941, when we got the news that the Japanese had bombed Pearl Harbor. Jay, along with some other young men in the choir, signed up to go to war.

I was so very grateful for God's intervention in his life, especially when I heard some time later that Jay had been killed in action. My first reaction to the news was sorrow, but it was followed immediately by rejoicing and praise that Jay was in heaven. The Lord had been faithful!

In 1942, Rev. Hastie scheduled a week of special meetings with R. D. E. Smith, pastor of the Assemblies of God church in Brainerd, Minnesota, and also presbyter of the East Central Section. Brother Smith stayed with the Hasties during that week, and I had much exposure to this godly man. He took a liking to me, and taught me how to play choruses using a few simple chords.

What I didn't know was that, as a presbyter, he was always on the lookout for someone who might be willing to pioneer a church.

Yet Another Sensible Decision

The presbyters for Minnesota were meeting, and the question came up—"Where should we start a new church?" R. D. E. Smith suggested the town of Little Falls. "I know a young man," he added, "who I think would fit up there. His name is Arvid Kingsriter, and I'd like to invite him."

"Arvid Kingsriter? He was a student of mine at North Central," said Ivan O. Miller, the assistant superintendent. "You write and invite him, and I will, too."

When I got the first letter from Rev. Smith, I felt a quickening interest. But a few days later, when I got a letter from Ivan O. Miller, I felt as if I were in a vise grip between the two men.

There were no woods available, I guess, because I spent the night earnestly praying and crying out to God for guidance by the furnace in Hastie's basement. I emerged for breakfast, and Mrs. Hastie asked if there was something wrong with my eyes.

No, I said, I'd just been praying about whether or not to leave Sioux

City and start a church in Little Falls. I wrote to the Minnesota brethren, telling them I would go to Little Falls and look the situation over before making a decision.

In the meantime, I happened to run into my brother Harland's brother-in-law, Ward Williams, who had pastored a Covenant church in Little Falls some years before.

When he heard I was thinking of starting a church there, he winced. "Don't go there," he said. "That community is almost 100% Catholic—you'll *never* make it."

It was an emphatic statement; I could have been intimidated. But I figured if God wanted an Assemblies of God church in Little Falls, then God would know how to make it happen.

Besides, to hear someone tell me I couldn't do something was almost like saying 'sic 'em' to a dog! So I decided I wouldn't let it bother me.

I was continuing to pray for guidance, but I was also gathering information. So I took the train to Little Falls and met with Rev. Smith. He took me around the town, and showed me a building we could use as a church.

Located at the corner of 3rd and East Broadway, it was a large, uninsulated wood frame building—basically a big shed. The seating for 500 people was made of ten inch planks with a six inch board for back support. The floor consisted of sawdust shavings from Larson Boat Works, spread over the bare ground several inches thick. There was a stove at each corner, made of two 50 gallon drums placed one on top of the other.

"All right," I said. "I'll hold two weeks of meetings, and then we'll see."

The Little Falls area had monthly fellowship meetings, in which various churches in the East Central section would get together for a Monday afternoon and evening service. R. D. E. Smith put my name in as the featured afternoon speaker, as a way to kick off the two weeks of meetings.

But I had already promised to play a trombone solo at the Sioux City, Iowa crusade for evangelical churches, the day before the fellowship meeting in Little Falls, Minnesota!

Not a problem, I thought with the optimism of youth. I called

Jimmy Nicholson, with whom I had traveled in the Evangel quartet, and he agreed to meet me in Iowa, drive us both to Little Falls, and help me by playing the piano for two weeks of meetings.

Jimmy and I drove all night long. It was a cold ride, since his heater wasn't working well, but we arrived in Little Falls in time for the afternoon service. I was tired, unprepared, hungry and unshaven, but the Holy Spirit came to my rescue.

The announced two weeks of revival meetings were uneventful, with attendance fluctuating between five and ten people. Jimmy Nicholson returned to Sioux City after the meetings were over, but I stayed on.

I'm not sure exactly when it happened, but gradually, over the course of the two weeks, I had come to a realization. Little Falls was the place for me, and pioneering a church was the work I was supposed to do.

Starting a Church from Scratch

R. D. E. Smith, with the financial support of his church in Brainerd, negotiated a one year lease on the large, unheated shed, with an option to purchase the property for $1,000. He opened an account for the new church at the American National Bank, and rented a room from an elderly Congregational couple who also agreed to supply my meals.

After two weeks of meetings, two women began to attend the services. I found out that one of them, Esther Anderson, had been praying for years that the Lord would send a minister and plant a full gospel church in her city. As soon as she heard of the meetings I was holding, she called a friend and invited her to attend. Within a few weeks, they had invited a third woman. So now I had a little flock of three.

My first challenge in pastoring this small flock had to do with my outlook on ministry.

When I agreed to pioneer an Assemblies of God church in Little Falls, I left behind a position as assistant pastor of a large church in Sioux City, Iowa. I had been working with a seasoned pastor who knew how to make decisions, and who was able to counsel me. Now it was solely in my own hands.

Move, and I Will Move

In the Sioux City church, there were hundreds of people, and I myself was responsible for about one hundred young people. In Little Falls, there were only three.

In Sioux City, there was a support staff and many volunteers. But now I knew I'd have to be not only the pastor, but also the song leader, pianist, treasurer, janitor—and woodcutter! I truly had to be 'all things to all people.'[6]

The day I visited North Central for an alumni function, and my former classmate ran up to me excitedly, saying that he had been elected pastor of a large church and was starting "at the top", I didn't know what to say. But after awhile, I was glad I had started at the bottom.

You see, I made mistakes. All young ministers do, but I found that it was better to make them in front of a few people than a big crowd. The few are usually more tolerant, forgiving, and less critical.

Attendees in larger churches have had mature pastors with ministries that have been honed through years of experience. As a result, the congregation expects the same level of maturity from successors.

People in small churches are often more patient with young pastors, giving them time to develop their ministry. Growth takes time in all of nature, and it also takes time for ministers to develop a mature presence.

The small church is an ideal place for a novice to practice and grow. Additionally, the pastor of a small church has the time to become personally involved with his people, so that he can monitor the circumstances that require personal ministry.

My classmate was not so fortunate as he assumed, when he stepped into shoes he could not fill. Within a year this man was asked to leave. He had split the church, in part because of his inexperience in working with people.

But I didn't know any of this, that day when my classmate was bragging. And when I returned to Little Falls from that alumni event, the three ladies didn't give me the red carpet treatment.

[6] Paraphrase of 1 Corinthians 9:22.

Starting at the Bottom

There was no promised salary. Being just twenty-one and single, I didn't even have a wife to encourage me; but I had the peace of God because I knew I was functioning in His will.

And when doubt would creep in, and discouragement was all I could feel, I quoted over and over to myself the 27th Psalm, which begins with these wonderful words:

"The Lord is my light and my salvation; whom shall I fear? The Lord is the strength of my life; of whom shall I be afraid?" and ends with good advice: *"Wait on the Lord; be of good courage, and He shall strengthen your heart; wait, I say, on the Lord."*

A Sunday or two after the alumni event, a big snowstorm struck in Little Falls. The house where I was rooming was a good distance from the wooden building we used as a church—over a mile—and across the Mississippi River. Oh, I was cold as I walked over that bridge, with the wind whistling over the freezing water! The temperature was below zero; I can only imagine what the wind chill must have been.

I got to the auditorium early and shoveled a path through the snow to the entrance. Then I started the fires in the four oil drum stoves with wood I had cut previously.

Although a thick layer of sawdust had been laid down, the ground beneath was frozen, sending up waves of cold. The auditorium walls were made of single boards with the studs showing. There was no insulation, for this structure had been built for summer use only by the Morrison County Evangelistic Association. Much of the heat from four crudely made oil drums escaped through those bare walls. It took a long time and a lot of wood to make the temperature tolerable for anyone who came to the service that morning.

After the stoves were blazing, I walked back to where I was boarding, had breakfast, and got dressed for church. Then I walked the mile back to the building to put more wood into those stoves and sat down waiting for the front door to squeak. That's how I could tell how many people came to the service. But that morning the door didn't even squeak once! So I had a prayer service by myself.

At noon I walked home for dinner and my landlord asked how the service was; and I said, "It was just fine!"

What else could I have said when the Lord and I had spent time together?

Move, and I Will Move

That evening I went through the same routine with the stoves, and shoveled another path where the first one had drifted shut. But this time, my three faithful ladies actually showed up, though they had to huddle close to the oil drum stove, keeping their coats and galoshes on.

This was the service where I started the women singing, then ran around, putting wood in the stoves—only to discover that they had dropped a key by the time I got back to the piano.

Now, if I had to do that today, I'd simply tell those ladies to wait until I could place more firewood in the stoves. But in my youth and lack of experience I thought that I had to keep the service going.

After the service, the ladies went to the back of the building and prepared to leave, while I counted the offering. It was all of sixty-seven cents. I went back to shake their hands, and one of them spoke up and said, "Pastor, don't you think we ought to give it up? It's no use trying to start a church in this town. There are too many Catholics here."

I responded with enthusiasm: "I believe the Lord is going to bless our efforts and people will come, and revival will happen."

She said, "I surely hope so!" and left with one of her friends.

But the third lady lagged behind to shake my hand. I felt her slip something in it, and as she shut the door behind her, I looked down to see a five dollar bill. God is still sending angels to encourage us!

The next morning I received a letter from a well known evangelist, inviting me to join him in conducting revival meetings by leading the singing and playing my trombone. I gave it some thought, but I knew where I'd been called. I wrote him and said, "No thanks. I'm real busy starting a church in Little Falls."

6
Compel Them to Come In

"Then the master said to the servant, go out into the highways and hedges, and compel them to come in..."
Luke 14:23a

That was a cold winter and a long one. After several months with just those three ladies, more started coming—but attendance really depended on the weather. That uninsulated auditorium was cold! Some folks came who were unchurched, and some from other churches: Baptist, Covenant, and Catholic. We still weren't running more than 15-20 on the best attended Sundays, but apparently even this small Assemblies of God church worried some people.

One day, a lay leader in another Protestant denomination asked to meet me for coffee at a restaurant. To my surprise, he tried to discourage me.

"Arvid," he said, "we've got this town covered. We don't need or want you to start a church here."

I realized that he didn't want more competition in a town where there were so few Protestants! I left that café praising the Lord that He was going to give us victory over all the opposition.

But there is more to victory than praising God. Jesus tells us through His parables that we are to act; we must physically go out into the highways and byways, and invite people to hear the good news.

But how do we do that effectively?

Move, and I Will Move

Listen to a Mentor

New pastors, because of their inexperience, are sometimes slow to recognize opportunities when they present themselves. This is when the counsel of a trusted mentor is invaluable.

I was not an experienced pastor at all, in the spring of 1943. It took the advice of a mentor to alert me to a wonderful opening for the gospel that had been staring me in the face.

Pearl Harbor had been attacked in December of 1941, a little over a year before. Our country had been plunged suddenly into World War II, and soldiers were going to nearby Camp Ripley for training before being sent to the war zones in Europe and the Pacific Islands.

In the spring of 1943, R. D. E. Smith, my mentor who had brought me to Little Falls, made a very good suggestion. Why didn't I offer my services at the camp armory?

It hadn't even occurred to me! Here were thousands of young men just ten miles north of Little Falls, about to be sent to war. They needed to hear words of hope and encouragement. They needed to hear the gospel. How could I have missed it?

But the moment Brother Smith called it to my attention, I knew at once that it was an excellent opportunity to minister. And as soon as I got home, I made the call.

I was connected to Lieutenant Heilbrum, the director of public relations at Camp Ripley. "Do you have a chaplain out there?" I asked.

Astonishingly, the answer was, "We don't have a chaplain for any of our units yet."

I told him that I was a local pastor, and offered to serve as the Protestant chaplain until one was assigned to the incoming units.

"I appreciate your offer," the lieutenant said. "I'll contact the Catholic priest in Little Falls, and if he consents to conduct Catholic services in the armory, you could do the Protestant services. I'll get back to you."

That very afternoon he called back and said, "We're ready to go."
"When?" I asked.
"Right away. This Sunday, in the armory."

Compel Them to Come In

In the church in Little Falls, I had begun experimenting with different times for services. Currently we were holding services at 2:30 in the afternoon, as well as 7:00 in the evening.

I had figured out that some people still wanted to attend their own church with their family and friends, but had a curiosity and a hunger for what was happening at our services. Afternoon and evening services gave them this freedom, and so for the time being, my Sunday mornings were open to hold services at Camp Ripley.

I had no transportation, so I arranged for a ride to the camp with the newspaper boy. I knew I could always hitchhike back in time for afternoon services.

At first, about two dozen G.I.s showed up for Protestant services. One of them could play the piano quite well. Another soldier, a sergeant, was an Assemblies of God brother, and he helped a lot.

On Sunday mornings he'd go from dorm to dorm where the soldiers were sleeping and shout, "Protestant church transportation will be here in thirty minutes."

Some Sundays, as many as six army trucks loaded with servicemen arrived at the armory for Protestant services. Some of them then got passes, and used their precious time off to attend our Sunday evening meetings in Little Falls.

Of course many soldiers got passes to leave the base, and hundreds of them would be roaming the streets of Little Falls on the weekends, looking for something to do.

I had something better to offer them than going to bars and getting into trouble! So, trying to think like my mentor, I actively looked for a way to reach out; and this time, I came up with an idea of my own.

The servicemen tended to congregate in the uptown area, and our church wasn't far from there. Why not put up something to ignite their curiosity, and bring them in?

I located a local sign maker, and had him paint a canvas sign that said "Servicemen Welcome." It must have been at least fifteen feet long, with big red letters. I put it up outside our building, and sure enough, in they came!

Sometimes as many as forty to fifty attended: privates, corporals, sergeants, lieutenants, and even majors. I kept seeing new faces, because men kept getting shipped out. I often wondered what God was doing in their lives.

Some of them corresponded with me, even after being sent overseas. This was an encouragement to me. I always did love to see the results of my labor, and those letters helped me see that the seed I was sowing was actually germinating and bearing fruit.

Go All Out

God wants us to go all out to bring people into the kingdom—but sometimes that can lead us into some strange encounters. I discovered this one day when a lady by the name of Dorothy Nichols came and asked me to engage her unsaved brother, Glen Muncey, in a boxing match.

Dorothy was a regular churchgoer, and she was very much in earnest; but even so, I thought this request was a little weird.

I said, "I'm not a boxer; I'm a minister."

"My brother thinks ministers are sissies," she said. "He told me, 'Go tell that minister of yours I might consider coming to your church if he and I could have a boxing match.' "

I was flabbergasted. I had no idea how to respond, so I stalled for time.

"I don't have any boxing gloves," I said. "And I wouldn't know where we could even have the match."

But she was ready with the answer. "I'll get you the boxing gloves, Pastor Kingsriter. And you can box right in my living room; I'll just clear the furniture out."

I didn't know what to say or do. In all my classes at North Central, not one professor had told me how to deal with a situation like this! But Dorothy was very persistent.

At last I remembered what the Apostle Paul had said in 1 Corinthians 9:22: *"I have become all things to all men, that I might by all means save some."*

With a stretch, I thought this could apply to becoming a boxer, at least temporarily. So I finally agreed, with great reluctance. But Dorothy was thrilled. She not only set the date—she even invited a few friends in to watch!

I felt very foolish. But I could hardly back out now.

Glen and I met, shook hands, and agreed to limit our match to three rounds of three minutes each. We put on our gloves and Dorothy rang a little bell to start the round.

Glen promptly hit me in the head.

I was shocked, and not a little dazed. The only boxing I had ever done was growing up on the farm with my brothers. Our rule was that we could *never* go for the head, and now I knew why—those blows hurt!

But I kept trying to be gentlemanly. I obeyed our family's boxing etiquette, and just hit Glen on the chest. Then he'd come back and aim for my head.

He hit me awfully hard that first round. Needless to say, I was getting the worst of it. But towards the end of the first round, it finally occurred to me that I didn't have to stick to any rules that Glen wasn't observing.

If Glen could hit me in the head, then I could hit him in the head. I knew that if I let things go on much longer the way they were, he was going to knock me out.

So I changed my tactics. I was taller than he was, and my arms were longer. By the end of the first round, I was landing blows that began to even up the fight.

Throughout the second and third rounds, Glen got a beating he hadn't expected. He was a good sport about it, though. After the final bell we both took off our gloves, laughed a little about the whole thing, and I left.

I have to admit, though, I resented having to go to such lengths. I didn't think it was right for him to have put me in that position.

But the next Sunday Glen was in church. I was surprised and overjoyed when he answered the altar call and gave his life to Jesus Christ.

After praying with him and rejoicing in his salvation, I asked him, "Glen, what was it I said in today's sermon that convinced you to surrender to Christ?" I figured, after all I had done to get him to come to church, surely I was going to get some of the credit!

But no. Glen answered, "It wasn't anything you said today. It was listening to the song that the girls' trio sang this morning."

I was humbled!

Meet People Where They Are

I was thankful that I never again had to box someone, just to get them to come to church. But I did keep visiting people on their own turf.

Little Falls was not a metropolis. It was a farming community. And, having grown up on a farm, my own heart was telling me that I could connect best with a farmer if I went out with him in his fields.

You see, a farmer is often quiet. But out in the fields with him, walking and working, talking comes more easily.

A man won't listen to you until he respects you. So when I showed that a preacher wasn't afraid of getting some cow manure on his shoes, they decided to listen.

There were times when I even helped them harvest their crops. And after awhile, some of them decided they could identify with me as their pastor.

Don't Neglect Visitation

It was a lot easier for me to relate to farmers than boxers, I can tell you. But no matter what walk of life people were from, I discovered that visiting people at their homes was essential if I wanted a growing church.

With a flock as small as mine, it wasn't hard to do frequent visitation. I tried to visit everyone weekly, and enjoyed these chances to connect with them on a more personal level.

But I also visited people who had never come to the church. Often a friend or relative of the person would have asked me to call, and I used that by way of introduction. This is the method that led to my one and only boxing match.

When new people visited our church, I'd make sure to get their names and addresses, and arrange to visit them in their homes the very next week.

Most of those visits were made at night when the husband, wife, and family were home. I'd learn the names and ages of their children, and showed an interest in their lives.

I always made it a practice of praying together with them about their needs and concerns. I usually made calls alone, even once I was married, because Marian would stay at home with our own children.

When, in later years, the church grew to the point that I wasn't physically able to visit all of the new people, I organized our church family to help with the follow up work in their homes. This was to take place early in the same week of their visit to the church.

However, I always visited personally when our people had to go to the hospital, or when they faced emergencies such as serious accidents, or loss of job. I'd go to listen and pray with them.

When a death occurred, I tried to give the bereaved a lot of personal love and care. I'd always be there to assist in making funeral arrangements, helping them to make contacts with an undertaker, or also with their loved ones when necessary.

I felt it was a privilege to be allowed to help people through the hard situations in their lives. Their problems and sorrows were all part of the work of a shepherd, and these difficult times made special links between us.

Stay Put

I knew of pastors that moved to another parish every time things got difficult. But when things got difficult for me, I often found myself singing the chorus by John Benson, *I Shall Not Be Moved.*

After I had been in Little Falls about four years, a respected mail carrier came to me and asked, "Arvid, how long are you going to stay in Little Falls? My wife and I would like to leave our old church and join yours for good, but we are concerned that you might move on to another pastorate."

I answered, "Alfred, what does it look like to you? I've been here four years, and I intend to stay as long as the Lord permits me to."

I discovered something wonderful through this. When I reassured Alfred of my commitment, he then felt secure enough in the church and its leadership to respond with a wholehearted commitment of his own.

In fact, he began to do some remarkable things. He took seriously these words of Jesus in Luke 14:23: *"Go out into the highways and hedges and compel them to come in."* Putting this directive into practice, Alfred began inviting some of the poorest of the poor to our Sunday School.

They were shabby and illiterate. But I felt good about having them in church. After all, when the disciples of John the Baptist asked Jesus if He was the promised Messiah, He said: *"Go and tell John... the poor have the gospel preached unto them"* (Matthew 11:4-5).

Those first years in Little Falls, I learned a lot about my part in the building up of Christ's church. I had to be willing to act on good advice. I had to go all out in my attempts to reach people, and meet them where they were. I had to earn their respect, and visit them in their homes, and care for them in crisis, and be committed.

Of course no church is ever built without the work of the Holy Spirit in people's hearts. But God expected me to give His work my best effort, and this is what I tried to do.

But I had many more lessons yet to learn. One of the most important had to do with money and my personal finances.

7

Faith and Personal Finances

"Bring all the tithes into the storehouse..."
Malachi 3:10a

"Give, and it will be given to you: good measure, pressed down, shaken together, and running over..."
Luke 6:38a

I was always an independent sort. I had been taught to work hard, to earn my way, and to save. But learning to trust God with my finances? That was an ongoing process. And it started with the example of my mother and father, and my very first lesson about tithing.

When I was nine or ten years old, my mother had me sit down with her at the kitchen table and laid out ten pennies in front of me. She said, "This is what you have earned helping me sweep the floors, Arvid."

Then she read Malachi 3:8-10 which teaches that the first ten percent of everything we earn belongs to the Lord. So mother removed one penny separating it from the other nine and said, "This belongs to God. On Sunday I want you to take that penny to church and drop it into the offering plate. You may use the other nine pennies as you wish. They are yours."

When Sunday arrived I carefully carried God's penny to church and placed it in the offering. That made me feel very good for two reasons.

Firstly, I felt good because I obeyed the scripture, and secondly, I felt good because now that penny was going to be used to bless the kingdom of God.

My father was also instrumental in forming my attitude toward giving. I remember so well that when our pastor, who raised chickens, would come to the farm to buy chicken feed, my dad would never charge him anything. He enjoyed giving the pastor a full sack, too. My father would fill the sack, then ask me to stand on top of the full sack and jump up and down, packing the grain tighter so he could get more grain in.

Dad was like that in everything he did; generosity was his trademark. If a board needed one nail to hold it in place, dad would always put in two or three nails to make sure it would hold. If he was working for someone else, and the agreed hours were eight in the day, dad would always put in an extra hour or so.

Some years later I was tempted to discontinue paying the tithe, and I began to experience some accidents which cost me more than the tithe I had been withholding. It was then that the Holy Spirit reminded me what His word said would happen when we robbed God of what is really His.

After giving it a lot of thought, I decided that it would be wiser to pay the tithe as soon as I was paid, rather than use it to cover the costs of unnecessary accidents. Ever since, I have not only paid my tithe to Him, but because of His blessings to me, I've often doubled and tripled the ten percent minimum.

Tithing is what God requires. But it is when we go over that minimum tithe that we are *giving*—and some wonderful blessings occur when we take that step.

God Rewards Even a Reluctant Giver

One October I had saved some money to buy a big-game hunting license. The deer hunting season would soon be opened and I was really looking forward to a hunting trip in the north woods.

Right before the planned trip, I attended a sectional fellowship

Faith and Personal Finances

meeting at the City of Lakes Assembly where a missionary was speaking. After he finished, the presbyter stood up and said: "I feel we should take an offering for this missionary so he can get back to the field of his calling."

Suddenly I felt the Holy Spirit nudging me to give the money I had saved for the forthcoming hunting season.

I wrestled in my spirit as the offering plate came nearer. How could I give up my annual deer hunt? Didn't God know how much I enjoyed it? And didn't I deserve a vacation, after working so hard for the kingdom?

But the Spirit kept saying, "Give it!" So I reluctantly reached for my billfold, took the deer hunting money and placed it in the plate as it passed by me.

I was left with mixed emotions. There was an empty and disappointed feeling, certainly. But on the other hand, I felt happy that I had obeyed the prompting of the Holy Spirit.

Several days later a friend gave me enough money to purchase the hunting license and buy gas for the trip. I got to go after all, and I thought that I would pay back the money later.

The opening day of the hunt was gloomy. As I walked through the woods in the rain, I suddenly saw an animal sneaking through the woods. I didn't recognize what it was, but I raised my rifle and shot.

The animal let out a blood-curdling scream that frightened me half to death. I couldn't see it running any more so I assumed that I had hit it, but I was afraid it was only wounded. Fearful that it might creep up and attack me, I waited for about thirty minutes, watching for any movement.

While I was waiting, the Spirit spoke to my heart, saying, "This is your reward for giving in that missionary offering last week."

I had no idea what that meant, so I finally decided to walk carefully toward the place where I had last seen the animal. My gun was at the ready; as I neared a crevice, I looked down. There it lay—a big bobcat!

I carried it back to show to my hunting partners, and they immediately said, "There's a bounty for shooting bobcats."

Before the day was over, we found a game warden. When he saw the animal he said, "That's one of the biggest bobcats I've ever seen. It's been killing lots of deer in this area. I can give you a bounty of $15."

That was more money than I needed to cover the cost of the hunting license and the gas for the car, combined!

I thought then that I had learned a valuable lesson about obeying the Holy Spirit's prompting, even when I had no idea how it would turn out.

Savings and Trust

I have mentioned before how, after graduating from North Central, I received letters from two different pastors asking me to become their assistants. One came from a well known pastor in Chicago who promised me a salary and benefits, and the other one came from Sioux City, Iowa. It invited me to come and minister there, but added, "All I can do is promise you room and board."

As I prayed about which offer to accept, I felt strangely moved to accept the one which promised only room and board in the pastor's home.

So I went to Sioux City, Iowa. There I learned a lot about ministry that became invaluable to my future effectiveness. After the first six months, Pastor Hastie gave me a weekly check of $7.50 which I exchanged for government bonds.

By the time I left Sioux City to pioneer a church in Little Falls, Minnesota, I had purchased enough government bonds to provide the necessary income to get me through that first winter.

During my first few months in Little Falls, my room and board was paid by the Brainerd Assembly. Later, as people began coming to the fledgling church we established, I received a weekly check of $15. This was enough for one person, with thrift—but not two.

I had a girlfriend I had been keeping company with for a long time, and I had given her an engagement ring. But I knew we couldn't live on only $15 a week. As I thought about that, I began to panic. I knew I had to find a way to earn some more money.

One day I noticed an ad in the local newspaper which offered to pay $5 for every cord of wood cut. I thought, "Hey, I own a double bit ax left over from cutting wood on the farm back home. Better yet, nobody from church will know I'm moonlighting, because I'll be out in the woods!"

So I drove out into the country with great anticipation, hoping to earn enough money so Marian and I could be married. The farmer directed me to the trees he wanted me to cut, and I began working right away.

The snow was almost a foot deep, so when I'd fell a tree it would almost disappear in the snow, but I didn't mind the extra work. I was young and strong, and I enjoyed the fresh air, and I really wanted to get married. I was twenty-three and had already waited for Marian four years. Marian was graduating from NCBI in the spring, and it was time.

Looking at Marian's picture.

That day I actually piled up two full cords of wood! I returned home, with the intention of going back to cut more wood the next day. But when I got to the house where I boarded, I found that there had been two phone calls from people needing my ministry.

The idea that I hadn't been available to minister, after the Lord had called me to do just that, really bothered me. In fact, I was unable to sleep that night because the Lord was trying to tell me that the woodcutting job was taking the place of ministry to people in need.

He challenged my priorities. As I wrestled during the night the Lord assured me that if I'd simply trust Him, and do His work, He'd provide enough money for me get married in the spring.

After resolving to trust God completely, I felt so assured that He'd take care of my financial needs if I'd take care of His work, that I didn't go back to cut wood the next day. I didn't even collect the $10 I had already earned.

And just as He'd promised, several months later Marian and I were married, and we were able to take a six week honeymoon trip to California!

My mentor, R. D. E. Smith, had phoned two pastor friends of his in Palo Alto and Modesto, California and recommended us to conduct two weeks of revival meetings at each of their churches.

The love offerings they gave us covered all expenses out there and back. And this time, I didn't have to play the piano with my own two fingers. Marian played beautifully, and it was a joy for me to see her at the piano, and know that we were beginning our ministry together.

God taught me a principle that year that has held true every year since. It is simply this: God can be trusted to take care of our financial needs, when we obey His will and trust Him to provide.

Addressing Personal Finances With the Board

Some years after I pioneered Bloomington Assembly of God (now called Cedar Valley Church), I encountered a personal financial problem which had the potential of threatening the health and growth of the church, and my own ministry as well.

For three years, my board had neglected to make any adjustments in my wages and as a result, I found myself in a perpetual financial squeeze.

The pressure was intense, and it was also getting into my spirit so much that it was affecting my ministry. I'd stand in the pulpit and have trouble preaching.

One day while I was praying about the matter, I felt the Lord give me a solution. He spoke to me suggesting that I prepare a list of all my expenses involved in pastoring the church, and then present the list to the board.

This list included my tithe, offerings, the cost of owning and operating my car, my house payments, my insurance, groceries, clothing, bicycles for our children, and gifts for our congregants' special events like graduations and weddings. At the bottom of the page, I totaled my costs of pastoring the church.

(Caveat: I don't recommend that every pastor should do this unless God specifically leads them to do so.)

Faith and Personal Finances

I called a meeting of the board and described my predicament. I showed them statistics describing the numerical and financial growth of the church. Then I said, "Brethren, I've been working very diligently to pastor this church, but for the past three years you have not made any adjustment in my wages. This problem has gotten into my spirit; and recently, I've not been able to minister without a feeling of resentment toward you. Please forgive me."

Then I gave each member of the board a copy of the list detailing how much it was costing me to pastor the church. After they examined the list, they asked me to step out of the room so they could discuss the matter.

I did excuse myself that one time, but since then, I have always insisted on staying with the board whenever the subject of my salary, or that of my staff, was being discussed.

After quite a while the Secretary of the Board called me back into the meeting. When I was seated, they all began to apologize profusely for neglecting their duties.

In essence they all said, "Pastor, please forgive us. We feel so sorry for neglecting our duties. We've been so busy taking care of our own situations that we've completely forgotten about you."

Then they said, "We've made a unanimous decision to adjust your salary to meet the total on your list beginning immediately, and we promise to consider adjusting your salary every six months from now on. We'll not allow this to happen again!"

Ever since that board meeting there has been a spirit of generosity that has prevailed in that church, not only toward their pastor, but also toward District ministries such as North Central University, Lake Geneva Christian Center, and missions, both home and foreign.

Throughout succeeding years, every time I'd see our church leading the state in giving to Boys and Girls Missions Crusade, Speed the Light, home missions and foreign missions, I realized it all began that night when our board decided to begin taking care of the needs of their pastor.

This may sound odd, but I really believe this was probably the greatest turning point in the history of Bloomington Assembly of God. When people establish a principle of generosity in their home church, it just naturally spills out into the rest of the world.

Teaching Generous Giving

I really become angry when I hear a minister approach offering time apologetically, as if giving in an offering is a painful thing to do. I've heard them say things like, "Well, I'll have to talk about the offering now," with a tone in his voice like he had to apologize for doing it.

In my ministry, I've taken just the opposite approach. I'm convinced that the Bible teaches that God loves the cheerful giver and that His blessings fall upon us when we are generous with our giving. I feel I'm doing the people a great favor by enabling them to become generous givers. I also feel that they will be better off and live happy and more prosperous lives by being generous with God.

One time I preached three consecutive messages on the subjects of tithes, offerings, and almsgiving. Surprisingly, the people ordered more tapes on these messages than any other messages I've ever preached. That convinced me that people really want to know what God's word has to say about stewardship and our personal finances.

But what about financial matters beyond the personal? What if we are responsible for other people's money, for the finances of the church? Can we, as leaders within the church, responsibly take the same risks with other people's money that we would with our own?

I think the thing to remember here is that it is, in the end, God's money we are talking about. And so the principles are the same. Work hard, be thrifty, invest, tithe, give; but ultimately trust to God's leading. If, after prayer and wrestling with God and counseling with other responsible Christians, you feel strongly compelled to move ahead and take a financial risk—then just do it. God controls all the riches in the world. He can certainly handle something like, say, a building program in Little Falls, Minnesota...

8
Building a Church on Faith

"But without faith it is impossible to please Him..."
Hebrews 11:6a

It was the autumn of 1943. The war was in full swing. And after nearly a year of labor in the vineyard that was called Little Falls, the fledgling Assemblies of God church was growing.

This was the heavily Catholic town where I had been told we would never make it, never establish an Assemblies of God church, never accomplish what God had called us to do. But when God calls us, He promises to move by His Spirit—and this was happening. People in Little Falls were turning out to be just as hungry for the experience of God in their lives as anyone else.

There was a pattern in God's dealings with me that I was starting to discern. I noticed that, once I understood His call or prompting in a particular situation, I would be met with an obstacle. Someone, somewhere would inform me that what I was trying to do was impossible. And if I followed through anyway, then very often I was hit with some kind of temptation to give up or turn aside.

It was when I had followed through to the best of my ability, and remained faithful in spite of obstacles and temptations, that God would invariably come through, often working through other people in ways that seemed nothing short of miraculous.

And this principle was never illustrated more clearly than in the early years of my ministry, as we tried to build a church to His glory right in the middle of Little Falls.

First Obstacle: Money

Attendance had multiplied from those first three faithful ladies huddled around an oil drum stove, to thirty or so on a typical Sunday. We were still meeting in the huge uninsulated wooden building, but my father had helped me put up a partition so the space wasn't so vast and echoing and could be more easily heated.

We would need a decent building someday. But in the meantime, the one year lease with its option to buy was running out on the current property.

It was a prime piece of property on the corner of 3rd and Broadway, close to the center of town. It was a wonderful site for our future church, but the selling price was $1,000. This was a lot of money in those days, and our little congregation wasn't rich. But we weren't going to be able to negotiate another lease, for we heard through the grapevine that there was an interested buyer waiting in the wings.

I felt that God wanted us to stay where we were. We were centrally located, and were doing a great outreach to the soldiers who came to town and saw our sign. I put the facts of the matter before the congregation.

There was only one member who had any money to speak of, and he generously put up $500. My parents weighed in with another $100, and between the rest of us we contributed the remaining $400.

I don't think anyone in town thought we'd be able to come up with the money. No one ever dreamed that our ragtag little group of 30, meeting in its temporary building, would find the necessary cash in wartime.

But we did. I still remember the attorney's face as I walked in to his office a few days before the option ran out, and handed him the money. He was not only shocked—he was irate. He was a member of the Catholic church, and he knew they were interested in that land. But he had to sell it to me under the terms of the lease, though he was clearly reluctant.

Temptation: Even More Money

As it turned out, the Catholic church was extremely interested in that land.

I used to get my hair cut at a certain barbershop in town. One day I was in the chair when a Catholic priest walked in.

"Would you be interested in selling that property?" he asked. "We'd pay $1,000 for it."

He knew what I'd paid for it, I realized. And I also understood that the attorney, a member of his church, must have been talking. The Catholic church owned property all around that piece of land, and when the priest was told that we'd purchased the land, he may have decided that he didn't want an Assemblies of God church going up there.

I told him no, we were not interested in selling.

"What if we offered $5,000 for it?" he asked.

"No, we're not interested."

"Well, what if we doubled that and made it $10,000?"

I was taken aback. This was fast dealing! Financially, it made sense for us to take the money, purchase a cheaper piece of property nearer to the edge of town, and build our church there. The delay wouldn't really matter, because we couldn't build anyway—building permits were frozen because of the war. Yes, it all made sense...

But no. This man's offers were only strengthening my resolve. God had placed us in the center of town. God was the one in charge here, and He was going to build His church no matter what.

I told the priest, "No—it's not for sale." And that ended it.

And a Miracle—For Someone Else

I was faced with an interesting and more subtle temptation about a year later, when Alfred and Inez Olson called me to their home.

Inez had just inherited $2,000, and they were interested in giving the money to foreign missions. Did I know of any foreign missions project that needed that money?

Oh, boy, I thought, we really need that money here. The temporary building we had come to call a tabernacle needed insulation, and the roof was leaking.

But though I was strongly tempted to ask for their money, I didn't. If God had laid it on their hearts to give to foreign missions, who was I to suggest something else?

"I'll research it and let you know what I find out," I said.

Now, some people might have picked up the phone and called around. That was probably the most logical solution. But I always liked to talk to people face to face, if I could. I felt that I got the straight story that way.

I wasn't married at the time, and had no family obligations to consider, so I promptly hitchhiked to headquarters in Springfield, Missouri, and spoke with Noel Perkins, our director of foreign missions.

"Just yesterday," he told me, "John Franklin, a missionary to Central America, came to me. He needs $5,000 to build a Bible school in Guatamala City. We could apply the $2,000 to that school, if you like."

I went back to tell the Olsons, and they liked the idea. And then I thought, why not let our congregation have a part in this mission, too?

So I told them about the need the next Sunday.

Would you believe it? God worked through us to provide a miracle for John Franklin and his aspiring Bible students. Our little congregation gave the other $3,000, and just like that, they had enough to build the Bible school!

Another Obstacle

I was thrilled that we had been able to fund the building program in Central America. But we needed to build in central Little Falls, too.

We could not begin any kind of building program, however, as long as America was still fighting in World War II. Most building supplies went toward the war effort, and building permits were still frozen.

In the spring of 1945, the war with Germany ended. In September, the peace with Japan was concluded. Meanwhile, Marian and I had married. Attendance at Sunday services was increasing, especially now that we had Marian as a pianist! But we both felt that the church would never grow as it could until we had a decent building.

By spring of 1946, things were loosening up. We heard that the government was accepting applications for building permits again, so we thought we should try for one.

At that time, Marian and I lived in a little apartment under the biggest beer sign in Little Falls. We lived on the edge of town, so all I had to do was walk across the highway and stick out my thumb. A Baptist man picked me up, drove me straight to the government building in Minneapolis, and even promised to pick me up for the trip back to Little Falls, too.

I walked into the office and said, "I'd like to put in an application for a building permit." The man at the desk didn't even want to take it.

"I've got a stack of applications this high!" he said, showing me a pile of papers three inches deep. But I convinced him to take the application anyway, although he said it was highly unlikely that I would get a permit within any reasonable time.

A Very Attractive Offer

A couple of months later I received a letter from Springfield, Missouri, offering me a job. It was a secure offer with an established church and a pastor that I respected highly—Emil Balliet, one of my instructors from North Central—and I was strongly tempted. I was at that time making just $30 a week, and Marian and I had no benefits, no housing allowance, and no car.

But one thing we knew. Money, stability, position—all meant nothing, if we weren't where God wanted us to be.

So we prayed. And we put out a fleece. We said that if we got the building permit, we would know God wanted us to stay in Little Falls.

And God Comes Through

My parents, Albert and Lillian Kingsriter, were running a resort in Park Rapids at that time, and they invited us out for a little vacation. We took the trip out with Russell and Fern Olson. On the way back, it was raining steadily. We were talking about the choice we had to make, and the fleece we had put out. I said, "Wouldn't it be wonderful if the building permit is in the mailbox when we get back?"

Marian said, "If it is, it's getting wet!"

The Olsons came with us to the mailbox. "Is it there?"

I didn't see anything. But after Olsons had driven off and we went up to the apartment, there in the stack of mail was a brown envelope marked "Official Business".

It was the permit! That was the first miracle.

The Pattern Repeats Itself

Well, now we had the permit—but we had no money with which to buy materials. God had given me a vision for a building, and we had had a builder draw up the plans, but we needed $70,000 to build the church we had in mind. So we tried to get a loan.

The banker said, "Give me the names of your people." He wanted to see if we had enough people to make a loan worth the risk—and if the people we had were solid citizens. Well, we failed the first test. By the fall of 1946, we had a congregation of about 50-60 people on a Sunday morning, but that just wasn't enough security for the bank.

Since we couldn't get a loan, we floated a bond issue to pay for the construction costs. It became my responsibility to sell the bonds, so I went around and asked to borrow money. I did sell some bonds, but very few people knew who I was.

The temptation is always to give up, but I was blessed with a strong streak of German stubbornness. I had heard that there was a farmer named Gage in Valley City, North Dakota, who had several children at North Central and was helping churches.

So I hitchhiked to Valley City. I didn't know how to reach Mr. Gage, so I just began asking around. Finally I found someone who directed me to his home.

It must have been early in the day when I arrived at his doorstep, because when I knocked and told him my errand, he didn't have his shoes on yet. He invited me in to tell my story, and began to put his shoes on as I talked.

But it took him a very long time. He'd listen to me, and stop with his shoe in the air, and look at it, and think for awhile. Then he'd ask me a question about the church and start to put the shoe on again. As I answered, he'd get to thinking about my answer, and pretty soon he was staring at his shoe again, not moving, just thinking.

He asked more questions—about the work in Little Falls, about my goals and experience, and all the time he was still trying to get his shoes on. But at last he was finished.

And wouldn't you know it, God spoke to his heart. Mr. Gage gave me a check for $5,000!

Never Say Never

We had enough money to start with, so I thought it was time to order some building materials. The Lord prompted me to contact the owner of Morrison County Lumber Company, a man by the name of R. D. Musser.

I was 24 years old and poor. R. D. Musser was a shrewd, powerful man, and a multi-millionaire to boot. Furthermore, his home was surrounded by a high fence, and there were guards on the property. Getting an appointment with him was more difficult than getting into God's presence!

I finally got an acquaintance of Mr. Musser's to intervene in my behalf, and was ushered into his large oval office. He was seated behind a vast mahogany desk, the very image of a man of the world. He invited me to sit down, and said, "What do you want, son?"

Well, I don't think I had any particular eloquence that day. I just told him we were planning to build a church—and then I asked what he would do to help us.

He paused a moment and then said, "I'll give you a 10% discount on all materials purchased through my firm."

Frankly, I had been hoping for more. But then he said with great finality, "I have *never* done that for anyone before."

I figured that it wouldn't be good form to ask him for 50% after that, so I just said "Thank you, Mr. Musser, and may God bless you!"

I'll never forget the first order I placed for building materials. The man at the counter was a deacon in a Baptist church in town—the very church which had sent another board member to take me for coffee and tell me they didn't need another church in town.

As I placed the order, I said, "I understand that your company will give me a 10% discount."

He gave me a rather superior look. "Oh, no. We never do that."

"But Mr. Musser told me that himself," I said.

Move, and I Will Move

"No, you've made a mistake. That *never* happens here."

"Sir," I said, "I'm simply following Mr. Musser's instructions. Maybe you'd better do some checking with your superiors."

The man, annoyed, left me standing there and went to another room. But when he came back he was shaking his head.

"You're right," he said. "You get the discount. But this has NEVER happened before."

This Time the Obstacle is Made of Brick

We had the land and we had some building materials. So we tore down the old wooden building, salvaged what lumber we could, dug a hole for the basement, and began laying concrete block.

The Congregational church in town opened their hearts and their church to us. They agreed to let us meet in their gymnasium while we were in the process of building.

But then came the news from Morrison County Lumber Company—there was no brick to be had, anywhere! Everyone was building, now that the war had ended, and the brickyards simply couldn't keep up with demand.

Oh, did we ever get ridiculed in town! There were people who didn't want us to succeed, and they made fun of us. You can imagine how humorous it would be—here we had this big hole in the ground, and no brick.

So we asked our people to pray; and I hitchhiked to St. Paul, to the Twin City Brick Company. They were Morrison County's supplier, and I just thought I'd talk to someone directly.

The man I spoke to shook his head. "I have a waiting list as long as your arm! There's no point in leaving your request. You'll *never* get it by the time you need it."

I said, "Sir, I've come a long way. And I have a hole in the ground and a group of people who are praying. I'm going to leave this request."

And the Wall Tumbled Down

It was only about a week until I got a call from the Morrison County Lumber Company.

Building a Church on Faith

The man on the line said, "Your order for brick has been approved, and they are being shipped."

He gave me the name of the railroad and the number of the car they were being shipped in—and then he said, "The man from Twin City Brick told me, 'Tell those people to stop praying. I'm having trouble sleeping nights!' "

I was so excited, I went down to the railroad yards on Saturday evening to see if it was in yet. I found the numbered car the brick was supposed to be in—but the yards were closed. I couldn't open the boxcar door.

Oh, well—I did just happen to have a crowbar with me! So I pried the door open just enough to reach in and pull out two or three bricks.

The next morning at church I said, "Folks, I've got some news for you," and then I held up the bricks. We were praising God for His provision that Sunday!

A Personal Hurdle

The owner of our apartment told us we had to find another place to live. He had heard that we were building a church that would include a pastor's apartment.

I've had an old tenant come back," he said, "and he wants your apartment. Since you're going to leave anyway, I'd like you to get out now so I can be sure to rent it to him."

The owner didn't know it, but Marian was expecting our first child, Kathy. I was feeling pressure to find someplace else that we could afford.

But we prayed, and pretty soon an offer was made. Dorothy and Jim Nichols had a winterized cabin on their property that we could rent at a reasonable rate. We were able to move in before the snow fell.

And yes—this was the same Dorothy Nichols that had once hosted a boxing match for me in her living room.

Yet Another Obstacle

That brick order had been approved so quickly, I hadn't had time to raise enough money to pay for the entire order. So I got another call from Morrison County Lumber Company, only this one wasn't as pleasant.

They said that unless they got their money in the next few days they'd put a lien on the property.

This temptation to despair was becoming familiar to me! But I knew what to do. Pray, and then get out there and see who God was going to use to help us this time.

Yet Another Miracle

So I went to another farmer that I had heard about, near Dassel. I walked out in the field to meet him, and he was plowing. He listened awhile, and then suggested that we go into the house to have dinner. I hope I didn't talk with my mouth full, but I know that I kept talking all through dinner.

After dinner he said, "Let's go uptown, and I'll get you some money."

We went uptown to an old furniture store that served as a bank and a mortuary, too. We had to walk past coffins to get to the safety deposit boxes—and he, too, gave me $5,000!

And God Just Kept On Providing

That wasn't the end of the miracles. Several times during the process of building, the lumber company threatened to put a lien on us because I hadn't sold enough bonds to pay for costs.

I continued to contact farmers with whom I was acquainted in Minnesota and North Dakota, talking with them out in their fields or wherever I could find them. God was always faithful in giving me favor with these potential investors, and I was able to secure enough resources to complete the church building.

And then we built that church with volunteer labor. I made a list of the volunteers, and posted it, with the number of hours each worked. Alfred Olson was at the top of the list. He was a man who loved to fish, but he didn't wet a line the whole summer of 1947.

The finished church included Sunday School rooms, a fellowship hall, an apartment for the pastor, and an auditorium seating 250 people. It served the congregation well for many years, and there is still a thriving AG church in Little Falls to this day.

You know, God almost seems to enjoy putting us in positions where we need a miracle—and then performing it. Perhaps this is His way of getting us to depend on Him. I know that my faith increased each time I had to trust God in a seemingly impossible circumstance.

Interestingly enough, the obstacles we faced mostly had to do with scarcity. And whenever I looked at my own scanty resources, I had a desperate feeling.

But God is wealthy beyond imagining. When we draw from His bounty, we really never have to worry about scarcity of money or materials. All that is required from us is to work faithfully, with patience and prayer. When we do that, God is faithful to speak to the hearts of the people He chooses, and we are given help for the next step on the path.

Move, and I Will Move

9

Leadership Lessons

"Remind them to be subject to rulers and authorities, to obey, to be ready for every good work, to speak evil of no one, to be peaceable, gentle, showing all humility to all men."

Titus 3:1-2

In the spring of 1943, District Council was held at Lake Geneva Bible Camp. I had taken advantage of one of the breaks to do a little fishing off the dock, when someone called, "Hey, Arvid! The presbyters just appointed you State D-Cap!"

D-Cap, or District Christ's Ambassadors President, was a position that I didn't know much about. I had never given it much thought, since I had been so involved with my church in Little Falls, but I was going to have to think about it now.

What is being D-Cap all about? I asked myself as I walked off the dock, fishing pole in hand. What am I supposed to be doing?

The previous D-Cap, I knew, was an evangelist who traveled a great deal. He had been unable to devote much time or attention to the job; I knew there would be no clear path or plan already laid out for me to follow.

I had no direction, and there were no seminars on youth leadership that I could attend, but I did remember having heard of such a thing as youth camps.

Move, and I Will Move

My mind was racing as I walked back to the meeting. Could we have a youth camp? Well, why not?

But I knew I would have to get the approval of the presbyters. And to do that, I had to have a good plan.

Two Essentials of Leadership

Without realizing it, I had hit upon two main characteristics of true leadership: the necessity of good planning, and respect for and submission to proper authority. In all the years of my ministry, I have seen over and over again that these two things are essential to the success of any dream.

But back in 1943, I didn't have a lifetime's worth of experience. I wasn't consciously thinking of these two principles. What I was thinking of was the presbyters. In particular, I was thinking of F. J. Lindquist, and how he would react.

Lake Geneva Bible Camp: the early years

F. J. Lindquist was a godly and great man of God. He was a powerful man of authority on the board of presbyters. He was also a little resistant to new ideas. If I couldn't sell my idea to Brother Lindquist, a youth camp was not going to happen.

Not only that, but I didn't want it to happen if I had to push it

Leadership Lessons

through over Rev. Lindquist's objections. I trusted his wisdom, and respected his authority. I had no intention of putting myself at odds with this man.

So if we were going to have a youth camp, I had to come up with a plan that would make sense to F. J. Lindquist. I had to get him to see the need of a youth camp, and show him a practical way to make it happen.

As I walked from the lake to the meeting place, I thought of Wesley Steelberg, and the pieces began to fall into place.

Wesley Steelberg was one of four assistant general superintendents in the Assemblies of God at the time. Each A.G.S. had a different area in which he specialized, and Wesley Steelberg's was youth. Marian and I had already heard Rev. Steelberg speak, and we loved his ministry. What an opportunity it would be for our boys and girls to hear this anointed man!

Even better, the presbyters had already asked him to be the speaker at our family camp in June. It suddenly dawned on me that, if Rev. Steelberg's schedule permitted, he could come three days early and speak at a youth camp as well.

It would be convenient. It would be a cost savings to hold the camps consecutively and use the same speaker. And best of all, it fit right in with what F. J. Lindquist had already approved! And by the time I entered the meeting place, I was ready with my proposal.

The reaction of the presbyters was very enthusiastic. And so in June of 1943 the Assemblies of God held its first youth camp at Lake Geneva.

We didn't have a lot of detailed planning for that first camp. We hired a lifeguard, I remember, so the kids could swim. But beyond that, there weren't a lot of youth-oriented activities.

It worked out, though. The kids made their own fun, organizing ball games and tag and everything else. The pastors and other adults from their churches came along and were counselors.

We had about 300 boys and girls, ages 9–17, and that first camp we didn't even separate the ages! But we held meetings, and there were good altar services, and it was a start.

In following years, we felt it wise to separate the camps into boys, girls, junior high and senior high. Each year, I would choose a camp director to head up the counselors and all activities—and I liked that. I liked to find good people, delegate, and then walk away and let them go to it.

Find Good People—Then Delegate

Here's how I would find good people.

I would first look for someone appropriate to do the job, a person who had a good record for the kind of thing we needed, and then simply ask him or her to get on board.

Almost always the person would say, "Sure." I never seemed to have problems getting people to take responsibility. But if they did say "No," I wouldn't beg them to reconsider. I respected their decision, and didn't even ask why. I considered that the person's own business, and none of mine.

It helped that people viewed my ministry as successful. That made people want to work with me; they knew they'd be helping to accomplish something. People are happy to spend their time and energy, but they want to see good results for their efforts.

In later years, I heard Dr. Paul Yonggi Cho, senior pastor of Yoido Full Gospel Church in Seoul, Korea, speak on this subject of delegating. At the time, his church had over 550,000 people attending weekend services. He said that his church was growing so fast, he needed a lot of people and pastors to help. He would go to them, and say that he'd like them to head up a certain area; and they'd invariably say, "I have no experience."

Dr. Cho would then say, "I'm going to give you experience!" He said that when he put people on their own and gave them total responsibility, they'd begin to pray, they'd get creative, and the results were great.

I found this to be true in my own ministry. When I put total confidence in a person and communicated that, the person in charge did much better than if I said, "I'll be checking up on you."

People have more ability than they know. If you give them total responsibility, *and don't take it away*, you can get wonderful results.

Leadership Lessons

Give Respect

Of course there are times when people do not live up to their responsibilities. I remember a time in Little Falls when a board member was in charge of the junior boys' Sunday School class. "I just can't handle those boys," he said once in a meeting.

I had already heard that there were problems, so I jumped on it. "I'll give it a try, if you like," I said immediately. And then I met with the boys. "Would you like to go squirrel hunting?" I asked them.

They liked that idea very much. So we went out in the woods, and found a tree with a squirrel hole a few feet up. The plan we came up with was that I would climb the tree and knock on the wood to startle the squirrels. The boys would take turns holding a gunny sack to the mouth of the hole, in the hopes that a squirrel would run into it.

We hunted squirrels all day, and never caught one. But the boys didn't seem to care; they had a great time. After that, the boys were willing to listen in Sunday School. You see, I had done something with them that *they* wanted to do, that *they* enjoyed. Since I had shown them that respect, they showed me respect in return.

I tried something similar in Sioux City, where I had responsibility for a group of young people who were kind of wild. I managed to arrange an outing where we played touch football; and that suited them so well. After that, I had no trouble getting them to do anything.

Winning Without Arguments

Well, showing leadership with boys and young people is one thing—but what about with adult leaders in the church, who want to pull in the opposite direction?

One of my earliest experiences with that was in Little Falls. We were building a church, and Marian wanted an organ. I brought it up at the board meeting.

A board member, a very opinionated man, spoke up at once. "I wouldn't give a nickel for a whole carload of organs!"

There was silence as the rest waited for my response. I looked down at the paper in my hand and said, "Well, what's the next thing on our agenda?"

Move, and I Will Move

I simply didn't respond, and he had no one to fight. There were no heated words slung around, no accusations or ill temper to cause bitterness later; and as a result, he didn't feel bound by pride to hold to his position.

Word apparently got around in the church. And two weeks later, a lady named Inez Olson came up to me after service.

"Oh, Pastor Kingsriter," she said with tears in her eyes, "we *need* an organ in our church! I will lend you the money for it, interest free, and you don't have to pay me back until you're ready."

"Sister Olson," I said, "will you tell the board what you've just told me?"

Well, those board members were still all there. I just asked them to step into my office. Inez, still sobbing, made her offer.

Amazingly enough, the man who wouldn't have given a nickel for a carload of organs two weeks before was the first man to make a motion to purchase an organ for the church. Sometimes, I would just win by losing!

That might seem opposed to conventional ideas of leadership. But I found it best to lead by gathering support rather than forcing conflict. And in future years, I developed a method of introducing new ideas that seemed to work well.

First, I would approach the person I judged was most positive about the idea. "I want to bounce something off you," I'd say, and ask "What do you think about this?"

Then I'd go to the person who would be the next most positive, and the next, and so on.

By the time the board meeting came, most if not all of the members had had some exposure to the idea, some time to think about it, and some positive thoughts on the matter. Then the rest of the members were often easily convinced to lend their support.

However, if there was definite disagreement at a board meeting, I would *not* call for a vote. I would say, "Let's think about this, and pray about it some more." And then I would bring it up at the next board meeting.

Planning Ahead

But how did I come up with these new ideas? Well, that brings me back to my first principle of good leadership—planning.

One of the first things I did as a leader was to plan ahead for each day, week, month, and year, and I'd do it in this manner.

First, I'd anticipate what was scheduled to happen in areas of my responsibility, plus things for which God had given me a vision. Then I'd make decisions about people who were involved, and who I should choose to help accomplish the desired goals within a particular period of time.

Next, during staff meetings, we would first pray together, and then we'd plan together, make decisions together, and finally write down notes about who was to do what, and when and how the tasks were to be done. The notes were important for clear accountability.

Further, as the leader of the staff and the church, I always felt that I needed to think ahead and develop myself personally. This would take the form of things such as consulting with successful leaders, attending church growth conferences, and praying for God's wisdom for the future. I read in a pastoral enrichment journal someplace that no church will grow if its pastor doesn't grow!

And finally, there was contingency planning. I took into consideration things that COULD happen, and prepared to make adjustments accordingly.

Submit to One Another

I never had much trouble personally with the second principle of leadership: respect for and submission to authority. But I saw the results where people did not take this principle into account.

We once had a director of our state's ministries who, when he came up with a new idea, would not consult with anyone, but would simply announce the changes he was going to make in the operation. Those in authority were surprised—unpleasantly so.

He was called on the carpet more than once for his tendency to dictate his plans without consulting anyone or going through the proper channels, and in the end this man was released from his position.

It wasn't that his ideas weren't good; it was that he did not have an understanding of how leadership functions. As a result, his good ideas seldom came to fruition.

But when an understanding of the principles of leadership is in place, all kinds of good ideas can be brought up, and hashed over, and made better, and ultimately put into effect. In the early 1940's, as D-Cap for Minnesota, I was given many opportunities to learn and practice these principles.

When the executives of the Assemblies of God decided to organize the youth of the denomination, they chose four Christ's Ambassadors state presidents to travel to headquarters in Springfield, Missouri, to partner with one of the assistant general superintendents and draw up a C.A. constitution and bylaws. I had the privilege of being one of this group.

We drew up the constitution and bylaws together, and then submitted them to the executives of our denomination for approval. These executives, pleased with our work, then asked us to come up with a program for young people to raise money for missionaries.

Our committee came up with the idea of Speed the Light, which was accepted and which has raised millions of dollars to provide transportation and printing presses for our missionaries to spread the gospel around the world.

It was exciting to be in on these decisions, helping to chart a course for the youth of the denomination or the church in Little Falls, and I was feeling more and more confident of my ability to lead.

Good planning? I could do that. Respect and work properly with those in authority? I could do that, too.

But as yet I was still a young and inexperienced leader. The denomination needed leaders far greater than I, to meet the challenges ahead. It needed men of stature and wisdom, men of courage and conviction, men who dared to stand up and speak the truth; and it would never need them more than in the late 1940's, when a spiritual movement within our churches went dreadfully wrong.

10

The Latter Rain Crisis

"...Do not despise prophetic utterances. But examine everything carefully; hold fast to that which is good; abstain from every form of evil."

1 Thessalonians 5:20-22 (NASB)

How would you like to be the one to tell people who were sure they had had a genuine experience of God, that the experience was false? How would you like to tell that to a whole church? Or to pastors attending a special council of the Assemblies of God?

That was exactly what had to be done in the 1940's, during what we came to call the Latter Rain Crisis. But it didn't start as a crisis. It began as a great spiritual revival, spreading to our state from Canada.

Canadian Christians were experiencing, under the leadership of an evangelist called Sister Beale, marvelous outpourings of healing and prophecy. An Assemblies of God pastor in Hibbing, E. M. Bloomberg, also known as "Mr. Gospel Radio," was strongly influenced by the teachings of this revival, and especially the idea of the latter rain, or latter day outpourings of the Holy Spirit, being greater than any that had gone before.

They quoted the phrase, "The latter rain shall be greater than the former" often enough that people began to call the revival "The Latter Rain Movement." The implication was that this phrase was taken from the Bible.

As E. M. Bloomberg brought in speakers from Canada, a similar revival took hold in his church in Hibbing. And at the beginning, much happened that was clearly of God. One of the more amazing healings was of a woman who had been born with a club foot and had never walked. When E. M. Bloomberg prayed for her, she was healed.

Other pastors in neighboring communities began to fast, pray, and bring people to Hibbing for services—and great things happened. But as District Superintendent Clarence St. John says about revival, "When something begins to happen that is unscriptural, watch out. If it's not dealt with, things get out of control."

The Focus Shifts

Gradually, the stories filtering back were less about healing and more about prophecy. And some of the prophecies, and resulting teachings, were very strange.

Many of these would come about during altar services. People would go forward for prayer—and someone who felt they had the gift of prophecy would lay hands on them, and announce that those who had come forward were called to go to India, for example. These people, who up until that moment had no sense of God calling them to do anything of the sort, and certainly had no training, would then feel obligated to quit their jobs, uproot their families, and go across the ocean to become missionaries.

Things got worse when a married couple would be prayed for separately. Off on one side of the altar, people were laying hands on the husband, and giving a prophecy that he was going to be a missionary in Africa. Over on the other side, the people praying for the wife would announce that she was called to go to South America.

Worse yet, a different woman was prayed over and told to go to Africa, and another man was directed to South America—and to solve the difficulty, a prophecy was then given that it was clearly God's will for the first couple to get a divorce, and marry their true "soul mates"— the other people who were called to the same mission field. Incredibly, people were actually getting divorced and remarried and heading off overseas as a result.

This was a revolt against all scripture and all common sense! But no one wanted to say that the prophecies were inaccurate. After all, if they weren't accurate, they weren't of God, and that was something no one wanted to admit.

So the prophecies were upheld by the leaders of the church in Hibbing. And the difficulty was addressed by using the "Latter Rain" doctrine. If the Bible said that the latter rain would be greater than the former, that was interpreted as meaning that a prophecy given in these last days was more important that any teaching that had come before.

But there was no such scripture in the Bible.

A number of verses about former and latter rains, referring to spring rains and rains late in the season, did exist. These verses all referred to both kinds of rain as needed for crops, and the latter rain was considered especially pleasant, coming as it did during a dry season. It was compared to a king's favor (Proverbs 16:15); it was withheld from the land when the Israelites had sinned (Jeremiah 3:3); and the people were told to pray for the latter rain for the grass (Zechariah 10:11).

There was even a prophecy about Jesus, comparing His coming to rain: *"...and He shall come unto us like the rain, like the latter and former rain to the earth"* (Hosea 6:3b).

And the only New Testament verse to refer to the latter rain tells us to have the patience of a farmer as we wait for our Lord's coming: *"Therefore be patient, brethren, until the coming of the Lord. See how the farmer waits for the precious fruit of the earth, waiting patiently for it until it receives the early and latter rain"* (James 5:7).

There was no verse that said 'The latter rain shall be greater than the former', but there was a verse referring to the temple that had just been rebuilt: *"The glory of this latter temple shall be greater than the former...and in this place I will give peace"* (Haggai 2:9).

Different verses, taken completely out of context, had been cobbled together; and the result was nothing less than heresy.

It was actually being taught in some Assemblies of God churches that a current prophecy would automatically overrule any prophecy, teaching, or law that had been given before—and that included the epistles, the Ten Commandments, and even the words of Jesus himself!

What made it so confusing for ordinary churchgoers was that the teaching, twisted though it was, had bits of truth and bits of scripture at its base.

In the hands of a charismatic and unscrupulous speaker, it all could sound very compelling. And no one could deny that, at the beginning of the movement, real miracles had taken place. Besides, pastor Bloomberg and the others were men of God, weren't they? Surely they wouldn't say it, if it were wrong.

It is a common tactic of Satan's to use a bit of truth in his lies. And that bit of truth makes the lie very hard to fight. The result was that people who stood against the wrong teaching, and the Latter Rain movement itself, were accused of being unspiritual, and of blocking a great work of the Holy Spirit.

This extreme doctrine was spreading throughout the Assemblies of God in Minnesota, causing great upheaval and concern. It became common, when pastors met, to ask "Which side are you on?"

And at last the issue became so divisive that our district leaders convened a special council to deal with the problem. Our General Superintendent, E. S. Williams, was called in to preside over the debate.

Two Leaders Stand Firm

During the first session of the council, the pastors were encouraged to testify about their experiences. Some testimonies were inspiring, and when they were given, elicited a loud "Praise the Lord!" Others asked questions about the scriptural warrant for the things that they claimed had been happening in their churches.

Someone mentioned that a young minister had received a call to become a missionary to China at one of the meetings. Since the person was in attendance, he was asked to give his testimony. This fellow was sitting directly in front of me, and he stood and gave an enthusiastic word about how God had called him to go as a missionary to China, and how he had been filled with the Spirit and then spoke in Chinese.

By the reactions of the assembly, and the conversations I had heard, I'd say the pastors were divided roughly in thirds. One third swallowed it whole. One third sided with the council leadership. And one third didn't know what to think.

At this point, F. J. Lindquist got up and went back to pray.

Discussion continued, and after awhile Brother Lindquist returned to his front row seat. "Is the young man who felt called to be a missionary to China still here?" he asked, standing and turning around.

The young man stood up.

"Now," said Brother Lindquist, "tell me. Have you studied the Chinese language? Have you prepared at all for being a missionary to China?"

The young man said that he hadn't studied the language, but he could speak it under the influence of the Holy Spirit.

F. J. Lindquist looked at him. "In that case," he said, "I command you to quote John 3:16—in Chinese."

Sitting behind him, I watched the young man's neck turn very red. Finally he stammered, "I—I can't do it now, but—when I set foot in China, I'll be able to do it."

There was utter silence in the room. The young man, his face crimson, sat down. F. J. Lindquist remained standing, commanding the room's attention.

Now, Brother Lindquist was a very strong, decisive man. He had the entire respect and admiration of virtually everyone in the room. After all, he had been the driving force behind North Central Bible Institute, Lake Geneva Bible Camp, *and* the Minneapolis Gospel Tabernacle, which at that time was the largest AG church in the state. Not only that, but he had begun all three in the middle of the Great Depression—and kept them all going! So he was well equipped for this crisis.

F. J. Lindquist

He let that moment of silence linger, as the foolishness of the young pastor's statement sank in to the room at large. And then he spoke.

"That's about enough of this nonsense." He glared at all of us in our seats. "It's time for the Assemblies of God to decide which way we are going."

His comments blew a fresh gust of common sense through the

room. And we all knew that his common sense was backed by a firm foundation of wisdom, proven works, and rock solid faith. I could feel the attitude in the room shift.

At that crucial point, E. S. Williams suggested that we adjourn, continue discussion over lunch, and meet back for another session at two o'clock.

But as we adjourned I noticed that F. J. Lindquist did not go for lunch, but went back and spent the time in prayer. Superintendent Williams also did not go to lunch; he retired to a little room behind the platform and began writing. And when two o'clock came, he was ready.

It was so quiet in the room, you could hear a pin drop. And then Brother Williams stood to read his opinion.

He commended the pastors involved for their desire for deeper experiences with God; but then he warned us to be careful that our experiences were supported by the scriptures. It was a well worded and powerful statement, and when he was finished, I could feel a shift in the room. I sensed an overwhelming acceptance by the pastors. And when the vote was called for, the Latter Rain Movement was rejected by about 90% of those attending.

The Rest of the Story

Pastor Bloomberg, however, did not accept the correction, and he left the denomination while continuing to act as a pastor. But in his refusal to submit to proper authority—first, the authority of scripture, and secondly, the authority of the church's governing body—he lost his influence for good, and went even further along the path of rebellion.

In the 60's, he began to proclaim that he would live forever in his present body. Later, he predicted that God was going to turn his aging wife into a "concubine" for him. When she died, he lived with a 25 year old woman without benefit of clergy, saying he didn't need to get married since the young woman was his reincarnated wife.

The sad thing is, this man was once a highly motivated spiritual leader, hungry for the things of God and to do God's will. He had had a powerful experience of God. But he let his doctrine be governed by his experience, not by scripture—and that is always a mistake. In putting personal prophecy above the authority of scripture, he was in serious rebellion, and he paid the price.

Tragically, many more people paid the price for this man's arrogance and rebellion. Marriages were broken, families were destroyed, faith was tarnished or lost entirely. And the Assemblies of God in Hibbing, under the leadership of E. M. Bloomberg, disintegrated as a congregation.

Years later, when a young man by the name of Clarence St. John went to Hibbing to pioneer a new Assemblies of God church, he had to work hard to overcome the lingering distrust that many felt for the Assemblies of God as a denomination.

Car repairmen insisted on cash up front, saying that Bloomberg had tried to drive off without paying. "God will repay you," he'd reportedly said.

A man who was invited to church by Rev. St. John said, "The last time I went to a church like that, someone ran off with my wife."

With labor and prayer, much of the distrust was overcome, and today Hibbing has a strong and vibrant Assemblies of God church. But the problem that cropped up years ago in the town of Hibbing still repeats itself in other towns today.

Whenever there is revival, there is a risk of the focus being on the manifestations, rather than on God. A true revival, a true movement of God, will never contradict scripture. There will be a depth to the teaching—it will not be shallow. And it will be subject to spiritual authority.

A pastor must spend time in the word of God and time in prayer, both in and out of revival. There are no shortcuts. And if problems arise, and they will, a pastor who is grounded in the scriptures will see problems developing, and move to short circuit them.

A pastor who is strong in prayer will be secure enough to withstand an accusation of being unspiritual, when he speaks the truth. And if he is firm in his faith, he will be able to speak, even if it means telling a whole roomful of pastors that they have gone down the wrong path.

It is wise to remember the history of our Christian faith and our denomination, even when it is painful. If it were not for the sound leadership of men like Frank J. Lindquist and E. S. Williams, the

Minnesota district would certainly have suffered a serious split in the 1940's. Other districts were also spared serious division in their ranks because of these men of God who held fast to the doctrines of the scriptures, and set the example.

11
Testing Prophecy and Guidance

"Beloved, do not believe every spirit, but test the spirits, whether they are of God; because many false prophets have gone out into the world."

1 John 4:1

I'll never forget the woman who came to my office one cold day in Little Falls. "Pastor," she said, "the Lord has revealed to me that I should leave my family and go into full-time ministry on the mission field."

I looked at her, astounded. She was married, with five children! On second thought, maybe that's why the mission field looked so appealing... but my job wasn't to analyze her, it was to guide her.

"Sister," I said, "the Lord can't possibly have told you that. It goes against scripture. The Bible tells us to bring up our children in the fear of the Lord... and how can you do that if you abandon them?"

On my advice, she went home and searched the scriptures herself. She couldn't find anything supporting her desire to leave her family, and she found many verses that exhorted her to take care of them. So she finally decided to stay home, and accept that place as her true mission field.

A pastor is responsible to God for his flock. When someone in the church is speaking questionable doctrine or prophecy, it is a pastor's duty to provide spiritual guidance.

But God does not throw us out there and expect us to just somehow know whether the spirit of truth or the spirit of error is operating through supernatural phenomena. He gives us a clear series of tests to apply.

Test #1: Is it Scriptural?

The first and most important test in all ministry and guidance is this; does it line up with God's word? This is a test that the woman in my Little Falls office did not meet.

The Bible is a yardstick against which we must measure ourselves. If someone declared that he was six feet tall, but when measured turned out to be only five feet ten, would he then cut down the yardstick or change the markings to support his claim? Hardly. And in the same way, we must be careful never to cut the scriptures down to our size, just to suit our own desires.

If someone is teaching something that doesn't agree with scripture, there is something wrong in the teaching. The word of God is our ultimate authority for all ministry and guidance.

Jesus himself, who often quoted scripture to make His point, says in John 10:35, *"...and the scripture cannot be broken."*

And Paul adds in 2 Timothy 3:16, *"All scripture is given by inspiration of God, and is profitable for doctrine, for reproof, for correction, for instruction in righteousness."*

So who are we to argue?

Test #2: Does it Glorify Christ?

If something is from God, it will glorify Jesus.

This is one of the primary functions of the Holy Spirit. In John 15:26 Jesus told His disciples: *"But when the Helper comes, whom I shall send to you from the Father, the Spirit of truth who proceeds from the Father, He will testify of Me."*

So if something exalts a human being, but not Jesus Christ, it fails this second test. There are Christian organizations and Christian workers that spend more time lifting themselves up than allowing the Holy Spirit to lift up Christ.

Testing Prophecy and Guidance

One day in the mid 50's, when I was on staff at North Central, we had a well known missionary evangelist to speak at chapel. I happened to be leading that service. During the prayer request time, I felt oddly led to request prayer for ministers and Christian workers that were exalting themselves and not Jesus Christ.

After prayer, I introduced our guest minister and sat down on a platform chair. The evangelist took the podium, turned, pointed a finger at me and said, "You don't know what you are talking about. You will be held accountable for saying that ministers are exalting themselves more than Jesus Christ."

I was momentarily in shock and hardly knew what to think. Had he taken my prayer request personally? Or was this a genuine prophetic utterance, and was I somehow in the wrong?

But as I sat there it began to grow clearer. This man proceeded to tell our student body, at great length, how very successful he had been as a minister of the gospel; and he failed to give the glory to Jesus for his accomplishments. Maybe he had been right to take my words personally.

He sounded, to me, like someone whose passion was to sell himself and his ministry, and not Jesus Christ. If prophecy is real and motivated by God's Spirit, it will center around Christ and lift up Jesus. True prophecy glorifies the Son of God.

Test #3: Is There an Inward Witness?

"The Spirit Himself bears witness with our spirit that we are children of God" (Romans 8:16).

And the Holy Spirit can give us that same assurance and conviction about other things, as well. When there is a prophecy, teaching, or guidance of some kind, the Holy Spirit will give a 'green light' to our inner spirit—a go-ahead signal.

The Holy Spirit, however, being the spirit of truth, also bears witness against or warns against fleshly operations in the ministry, as well as demonic spirits operating through a ministry. Such warnings signal a yellow or red light by an inward witness.

One night while traveling with the North Central male quartet, I was preaching to a congregation I'd never met. Right in the middle of

Move, and I Will Move

my message, a person entered the service and sat down. All of a sudden my throat felt as if someone were choking me, and I had great difficulty continuing the message. My inner spirit told me that the person who had just entered the service had a demonic presence, and was trying to stop my preaching. I paused briefly, and quietly rebuked that spirit. Immediately I felt a great freedom and continued preaching.

After the meeting I related my experience to the pastor and he said, "That person is known to be demon possessed, and we've been praying about how to deal with it." I was frightened to think that demons possessed the power to paralyze me and stop me from preaching—and awed at the power of God, which was even greater.

When things are not right, when they are out of line, you know it by the inward witness. When things are right and of God, you also know this within your heart, by the Holy Spirit's witness.

One day in Little Falls, I was cutting wood to heat our church, a large wooden structure meant for summer meetings, and praying about our need for a new building. I sat down on one of the felled trees to eat my lunch, wondering how large a new church should be, how it should look, and how many rooms we would need.

Suddenly God gave me a vision in my spirit of a church building that fulfilled all our needs. I got so excited that I threw my ax into the trunk, raced home, and began drawing prints of what I had seen in my vision: a sanctuary seating 250 people with a balcony, plus a two story

Little Falls Assembly of God Church: the vision became a reality

educational building that held classrooms, a prayer room, an apartment for the pastor, and an office. Along with the vision, I experienced an inward witness that it was the right thing to do—and it was. God's blessing was upon the entire building project in Little Falls, and the congregation continued to grow as we obeyed that inner witness which revealed His will and the needed direction for the future.

Test #4: Does it Produce Liberty and Peace Instead of Bondage?

If something is from God, it will lead us into freedom. Jesus has come to set us free, and all true ministry which has God as its source will bring us into liberty.

The apostle Paul wrote in Galatians 5:1: *"Stand fast therefore in the liberty by which Christ has made us free, and do not be entangled again with a yoke of bondage."*

A spirit of bondage comes from Satan and is often produced when the flesh decides to control things which only God's Spirit should control.

One day, while pastoring in Little Falls, a letter came inviting me to be the song leader for a missions convention at a large church in Ohio. The speaker was one of the most respected missionaries in our movement, and after praying about it, I felt a release to accept. But during the second day, when we were in a prayer meeting, I felt a hand on my shoulder. The missionary convention speaker said, "Brother Kingsriter, I've received a word from the Lord. He wants you to accompany me when I return to Borneo this year."

I had no thought of ever going as a missionary overseas—and I didn't even know where Borneo was! I said, "Brother, I don't feel that's what the Lord wants me to do with my life right now."

He said, "Please pray about it," and left me.

I was confused. I sincerely wanted to do what God wanted me to—but the Lord hadn't spoken to me about this at all. I continued to pray, but the missionary's "word" was very threatening to me. I was miserable the rest of the convention. I even wrote my fiancée, asking her to pray for me, that I would make the right decision. I finally told the Lord, "I'll go to Borneo if you want me to."

I was serious! I had made the commitment. And the moment I said, "Yes, Lord, I'll go if you want," He poured His peace into my heart. The entire issue disappeared and has never surfaced again.

Looking back on that experience, it dawned on me that God was testing my willingness to change the course of my life, if He wanted me to do so. Confused and threatened though I was, total surrender to God's will, whatever it might be, produced in my spirit unmistakable liberty and peace.

God may have been testing my willingness to follow Him through the word from this missionary, but it is important to remember that God had not spoken to me about it. If someone else says they have a word from the Lord about you, that is never enough to go on. God will speak to your own heart first and foremost about any plans He has for you. The true "word from the Lord" generally acts as a confirmation of something that God has already revealed to a person.

Test #5: Is the Fruit of Life and Ministry Good?

Jesus taught that if something is of God, the fruit will be good, and if it is of Satan, the fruit will be blighted. Jesus warned, "Beware of false prophets, who come to you in sheep's clothing, but inwardly they are ravenous wolves. You will know them by their fruits" (Matthew 7:15-16).

The Latter Rain Movement brought with it some good fruit at its outset—but in the end, the prophecies were false, the fruit was blighted, and many lives were damaged.

The early church must have had some problems with false prophecy too, because John wrote: *"Beloved, do not believe every spirit, but test the spirits, whether they are of God; because many false prophets have gone out into the world"* (1 John 4:1). And false prophecy continues today, in various forms and under many disguises.

People sometimes think they have a word from God when they really don't. Perhaps they have an overactive imagination. Perhaps they want attention and are deceiving themselves. Perhaps they lack experience in discerning the voice of God, and are the type to charge ahead anyway. Whatever the case, the results can be funny at best, and deeply harmful at worst.

Jac Perrin, pastor of Eden Prairie Assembly of God, tells the story of a married friend of his who wore no wedding ring. Jac and his friend, both students at North Central, were stopped in the halls one day between classes by a rather intense young woman.

She pointed a finger at Jac's friend Ed and said loudly and authoritatively, "Stop right there! I have a word from the Lord for you!"

The crowded hall went suddenly silent, and a ring of students formed around the little drama. The woman stepped forward, cheeks flushed.

Jac remembers thinking, "Wow! God is giving Ed a word just for him!"

And then the woman poked Ed in the chest with her finger, and said, "You are going to marry my roommate!"

Jac saw his friend's eyebrow go up, and the right corner of his mouth twitch just slightly.

"Well, that's fine with me," said Ed slowly. "I want to please God in everything I do. And I'm okay with it, as long as God tells my wife."

The whole crowd was chuckling as the woman stiffened, whirled around, and disappeared into the crowd. But funny as it was, Jac said you could tell the young woman had really believed it.

This happens sometimes when people are trying to learn the difference between their own imagination, and the Spirit of God. So if anyone feels they are getting a word from the Lord, the first thing to do is to ask God if you're supposed to share it. Ask this many times, over a period of time. Because sometimes you may get a word like this, but it's not for you to share; it's so you can be in prayer for them, and minister to them without confrontation.

But if you do think you are supposed to share, never try to come across like some Old Testament prophet saying, 'Thus says the Lord!'

I would suggest that if anyone feels they have a true word from the Lord about someone else, they should phrase this very carefully. Speaking quietly, in private, and using phrases like "I believe I may possibly have a word from the Lord about you; would you like to hear it?", or "You know, it might just be me, but I was praying and I got a picture just now about you, and I think it may be from the Lord—would you like me to share it with you?" is not just beating around the bush. An approach like that is simply a gentle and courteous way of introducing what, by its very nature, must be an intensely personal communication.

And then, if they allow you to share it, it is good to ask "Do you think that might have anything to do with your situation?", or "Does that mean anything to you?"

You will discover very quickly if you truly have passed on a true word from the Lord. Oftentimes people can't even respond, because the confirmation they just heard from your lips causes them to weep.

We can't see on the surface a person's motivations or which spirit is energizing someone's ministry, but we can test and know whether or not a person's ministry is of God. Jesus said we could recognize a true ministry by its results.

If a ministry produces discord, dissension, division and rebellion, you can be sure it's not of God. If it produces unity, love, peace and faith, you can be assured that God is at work.

Test #6: Does it Come to Pass?

The enthusiastic man stood up in the middle of the church service and raised his voice to prophesy. There would be a great earthquake in California, he said, and the city of San Francisco would fall into the ocean. It would happen that month, he said—and he named the date!

I was just a teenager in our little Paynesville church, and I was frightened. I hadn't read the paper, and so I didn't know that the man was just repeating what he had read in a newspaper column. It sounded real enough to me—and to some other folks too, I'd guess.

But Pastor Klingsheim was grounded in the word of God. After the service, he asked the man to come to a back room to meet with the board. My father, a board member, told us later what had happened.

"You may have thought that was a genuine prophecy," said the pastor, opening his Bible, "but it wasn't scriptural. First Corinthians 14:3 says, *'But he who prophesies speaks edification and exhortation and comfort to men.'*" Pastor Klingsheim spoke kindly and firmly. "Your so-called prophetic utterance didn't do any of those things, and we ask that you don't do that again."

The man apologized, and asked the pastor and board to forgive him. They then laid hands on him and asked that God's Spirit would give him the true gift of prophecy.

I have to confess that, on the date the man had named, I did wonder if anything would happen. And when the day passed with no earthquake, I was relieved—and thankful that my pastor knew the scriptures well enough to test the "prophecy."

When someone gives a prophetic utterance which is of his own making, and not of God, he is seeking to deceive his hearers to believe it is God speaking through him. Scripture warns of the danger of deception... of humanly faking what is genuinely the prerogative of the Holy Spirit.

And if we were to go by the Old Testament law, in Deuteronomy 18:20-22, the prophet whose words do not come to pass would be put to death! So it is a serious thing.

More Thoughts on Prophecy

We do not want to quench the Spirit of God—we want the gifts of the Spirit to be used freely in our churches. But it is important to be aware that whenever there is a move of the Spirit, there will also be spiritual opposition, aimed at getting people off track. And, as my wife Marian says, "If Satan can't make you stop believing, he'll try to make you unbalanced."

Sometimes people get a little ridiculous. What they think is prophecy is nothing more or less than an overactive imagination.

There was a fellow I knew once who was filled with the Spirit in church, and he was so excited and inspired that he came up with what he thought was a great plan. He thought I should go on the road with him; that we should travel together and do evangelistic work. And he was no more fitted to do anything of the sort than anyone else you'd run into on the street.

But I found that, when people went off the track, sometimes just not responding at all was enough to let them know that I didn't approve. If I didn't comment for or against what they proposed, that sometimes had greater influence than if I had responded.

Of course I had a responsibility to teach. But the way I addressed imbalance in the church was usually via the pulpit. I'd wait till I felt it was an appropriate time, and then I'd teach from the scriptures—something to get people back on solid ground.

We pastors have an advantage, because in our society no one interrupts us when we're preaching. You can be challenged in a Sunday School class... but in the pulpit, you've got 'em for the duration. I found that I did most of my counseling from the pulpit!

To sum up, it is important to realize that if God is guiding us, the guidance will be scriptural, and we will have an inner witness and peace in our heart that it is God. God will provide where He guides. And ultimately, though not always immediately, circumstances will open up as we walk in faith.

As I look back on my life and ministry, I do not recall times when the church as a whole got really off base. I took as my doctrine the verse that tells us to teach here a little, there a little, line upon line, precept upon precept[7], and so with a slow but steady building up of teaching and character, the church body was continually being brought to maturity.

'Slow and steady' seem to be two words that characterize my experience. As I look back, I do not recall that the churches under my ministry ever experienced a sweeping revival.

There were times, of course, where there was a greater movement of the Spirit than others. God is at work in our hearts all the time, working to draw us closer to Him and His kingdom purposes. Periodically, we may experience an inner urging to seek God with a new fervor; this is a kind of revival.

But in order to discuss significant community-wide revival in Minnesota, I have to look to other pastors: F. J. Lindquist, for one, and my own father-in-law, James D. Menzie.

---

[7] Author's paraphrase of Isaiah 28:10.

12

Casino Revival

"The harvest is past, the summer is ended, and we are not saved!"
Jeremiah 8:20

It started with three women on their knees.

The year was 1921, and the place was Casino, Minnesota: a sparsely populated group of farms about ten miles north of Pillager, in the beautiful north woods. The name, locals say, came about because there once had been a gambling casino there.

The casino was no longer there in 1921, but the legacy of hard living and hard drinking had continued. Godly farmers who had settled the area found that their children were running with a rough crowd. And so three women—Helen Horn, Mrs. J. Raymond Martin, and Ida Peterson, began to pray. They prayed for their children, and for their community. They prayed for revival.

And God, who loves to answer prayer, had already begun to work in the lives of two young men who would answer the call.

Revival's Roots are in Prayer

A young man by the name of Frank J. Lindquist, at age 16, had attended Pentecostal meetings in McKeesport, Pennsylvania, and was saved and filled with the Holy Spirit. As a youth, he worked first in the steel mills, and then got a job in the dairy business—at the Menzie Dairy.

Move, and I Will Move

The Menzie Dairy was run by two brothers, John and James. Their mother, a godly Scotchwoman, had offered each of her sons a reward of $500, saved from her egg money, if he got to the age of 21 without ever once smoking or drinking.

She prayed for all her children, but she had a particular prayer that was very close to her heart. She prayed that God would call one of her sons to the ministry. She did not tell anyone of this prayer of hers at the time, trusting to God to do the influencing.

When Frank Lindquist came to work at the Menzie Dairy, he felt a concern for his employers, and began to pray for their souls. He talked about the Lord on the job, and invited the Menzie brothers to meetings at the Casley brothers' mission.

John was converted first, and then James. John continued in the dairy business, but James felt a powerful call of God to give up the business where he had been so successful, and preach the gospel. When he shared this news with his mother, she began to cry. "I prayed for this," she told him.

James D. Menzie, age 21

Revival Requires Sacrifice

James spent a year at a seminary in New York. When he came back, he spoke with evangelist Ben Hardin. "You've traveled a great deal," James began. "Where, in your opinion, do people need the gospel the most?"

Ben Hardin answered, "Northern Minnesota."

This was James Menzie's call, and he knew it. But such a mission would cost money. Who would buy the tent needed to hold meetings where there were no churches? How was he to travel, to eat, to live?

It was impressed upon James that he, himself, had the money. He had done very well in business in the few years he had partnered with his brother. He also had the $500 his mother had given him at age 21.

But he came from a thrifty, tight Scotch family. Money—the making of it, and the keeping of it—was a major topic of conversation when all

Casino Revival

the relatives got together. Money was not lightly spent on anything that wasn't an absolute necessity.

Slowly James began to feel that money had held an all too great place in his life. He had to consecrate that part of his life to God. And so he decided to use all his money to finance the trip.

He asked Frank Lindquist to come with him. And so they bought a truck, packed it full with a 40' x 60' tent, folding benches, stakes, rope, and poles, and headed to northern Minnesota to find a needy community.

In those days there were no motels. One night they even had to sleep in an empty chicken coop. The roads were poor, mostly dirt or gravel, and there were few route signs. But they made it to the Brainerd area by the fall of 1921, and began to look around for a place to hold meetings.

November 24th, 1921: James D. Menzie and F. J. Lindquist out prospecting for places to hold meetings.

Their first meeting was in Staples, Minnesota, where they spent about four weeks with some success. In September of that year they also began tent meetings in the Brainerd and Crosby-Ironton areas.

Around Thanksgiving, James Menzie was invited to visit in a home in Staples. The lady of the house, Mary Horn Bryant, said that she had been praying for family members in Casino. Would James consider holding meetings there, too?

James promised to pray about it and discuss the need with Frank Lindquist. And they did.

But winter was already upon them. James and Frank quickly discovered that northern Minnesota was *cold*. Tent meetings were not possible in weather that was an astonishing 25 and more degrees below zero. The roads were unplowed, and impassible except by sleigh. So James and Frank took the train, and walked miles from the station stops to the backwoods communities.

Tent meeting, James D. Menzie preaching; attendance was sparse at the beginning. The sign reads, "What Shall I Do Then With Jesus Which is Called Christ?"

While continuing to hold services in the surrounding areas, they began to also hold meetings in a little country schoolhouse in Casino called Sunrise School. The three praying women were among the first to attend, and soon there was a small group of believers meeting.

But the group stayed small. All through the winter and spring, the young evangelists preached the gospel in Casino, and saw very few results. But although they could have been discouraged, and no doubt were at times, they remained faithful.

On June 4, 1922, the young preachers pitched their tent in a wooded area near Axel Peterson's farm, and began to hold meetings. And on June 25th, the earnest prayers of three women, and those others who had begun to pray with them, were answered.

Revival Happens When the Spirit Moves

The text on June 25th was from the eighth chapter of Jeremiah: *"The harvest is past, the summer is ended, and we are not saved!"* James Menzie preached, and an invitation song was sung.

It is worth noting that James D. Menzie was not a particularly emotional or charismatic preacher. He always spoke quietly, in a measured tone, and this evening had been no exception.

Casino Revival

But this night, as the young preacher knelt to pray, the Spirit of God swept across the meeting place.

Suddenly Thomas Horn was on his back at the altar, praying in a loud, clear voice. Someone else began speaking in tongues. Emory Horn walked up to the altar to look at his brother, and in a moment dropped to his knees and began crying to God for salvation. After a time he sat up, began praising God in another tongue, and then walked out through the tent flap so that he could continue praising God under the open sky.

A conviction of sin was heavy upon the whole room, according to those who were there. People began to cry for mercy, confessing their sins, and at the altar many were baptized in the Holy Spirit. Two more of the Horn men, Raymond and Wilmer, were saved—all relatives of Mary Horn Bryant, who had prayed for them.

Christians looked on with praises to God, while according to witnesses, the non-Christians were apparently terrified. Thomas Horn arose to his feet and began to warn and exhort sinners to come to Christ. Ada Peterson, Ida's daughter, was also on her feet, pleading for sinners to open their hearts to Christ. Raymond, Wilmer, and Helen Horn were all talking personally to those yet unsaved. Several others were saved and filled with the Holy Spirit.

A young man at the back, who had come to make fun and disrupt the proceedings, was the last one to come forward. He knelt by the altar

The tent was set up in a field or vacant lot with the permission of the owner. The sign reads, "Come and hear the Lady Evangelist, Miss Ada Peterson. Bring the sick to be prayed for."

and received God's forgiveness, and the meeting was closed by Ada Peterson at 1:00 am.

Revival fires, once lit, spread throughout the whole community. But, as in any move of God, there was opposition.

Some of the young men were angry that their girlfriends had become Christians and weren't willing to run around with them anymore. They began with ridicule, laughing at those who attended the meetings. When this didn't work, they began to puncture tires and take parts off cars that were parked by the tent. Next they threatened to destroy the tent itself, and even to tar and feather James and Frank and ride them out of town!

James was concerned about the safety of the tent, and slept in it to guard it. But acid was thrown on the tent, eating through the fabric and ruining the piano behind.

This only made the converts more determined. They said, "We're going to have a church—our own building, right here!"

Axel Peterson, a farmer and staunch Christian, donated the land for a permanent building, and the foundation was poured. In the meantime, his wife Ida, one of the original praying women, offered to take James Menzie into her home so he could be close to the tent without having to actually sleep there.

Many worked hard to erect the new church, and the building was completed by fall of the same year, 1922! (And a personal footnote to this story is that Axel and Ida Peterson had another daughter, Agnes, who married James Menzie in 1924, and became the parents of my wife, Marian.)

Revival Has a Purpose

Revival is an exciting word. The Spirit of God sweeps across a church, a community, even a nation, kindling hearts to flame. People weep, cry out, praise God, speak in other tongues. There is prophecy and healing and anointed preaching. Personal ambition is placed on the altar, and busy and productive people put their lives on pause in order to wait before God, receive His gifts, and discover His will for their lives.

Still, every revival has an end. The day of Pentecost must have been an incredible time, with thousands coming to Christ. Imagine the

Baptismal service at a lake near Brainerd, Minnesota.

baptisms, the small groups springing up in every home, the power of the Spirit loose in that community! It must have been cataclysmic.

But the time of total immersion in the Spirit, of joyfully receiving everything God had to offer and thinking about nothing else, came to a close. I wonder how the disciples and all those new believers felt. Had they wanted it to go on forever? Did they feel abandoned, bereft? Did any of them feel that they had somehow lost God, and pray louder and cry harder, trying desperately to get that first euphoric feeling again?

Some, perhaps, did. But the more sober and mature Christians there understood that God was still present—and that the revival, the flames of Pentecost, had come for a purpose. And that purpose was power.

What good is it, if we keep charging up a battery, but never use it to start the tractor? If the tractor had feelings, it might love the sensation of being charged—it might feel joyful and flooded with power—but unless it gets to work and starts to pull a plow, or haul some logs, that power is wasted.

It is the same for us, here and now. When God sends revival, whether to an individual heart or to a church or to a whole community, it is for a purpose. And the test of that revival can be found in what remains behind when the revival has passed. What is left that is lasting? What is left that continues on?

The Fruit of Revival

A church was not only built in Casino, but also in Brainerd, Motley, Staples, and Crosby-Ironton: every community where Frank Lindquist and James Menzie held tent meetings formed a permanent church.

Casino Assembly of God Church, fall of 1922

But it was clear to the two men that all these new churches needed some sort of overseeing body. The Holy Spirit was sweeping not only through the town of Casino, but in towns and cities all across the nation. People who were being filled with the Spirit and speaking in other tongues were being told to leave their churches—but under what denomination could they organize?

It was important, these evangelists knew, that churches be under some kind of authority. This was biblical, and necessary to prevent excesses or wrong doctrine from taking hold.

Not only that, but they had come to realize that they personally needed to subject themselves to authority. So far, James Menzie and Frank Lindquist had no credentials at all. Neither one had been ordained, or even had a license to preach.

And so, in 1922, they planned a ministerial convention.

The convention was to be held at the Brainerd church. Frank Lindquist and James Menzie invited E. N. Bell, an official of the General Council of the Assemblies of God with headquarters in Springfield, Missouri, to speak. Ministers from all over the Midwest attended.

The problem of ordination for James and Frank was quickly solved. E. N. Bell simply said, "We see here the evidence of their calling. They have built a church, they have organized a congregation, and they clearly have a Spirit-empowered ministry. So why not ordain them?"

Casino Revival

The other officers who came with him from Springfield agreed, and so James Menzie and F. J. Lindquist were ordained as ministers of the Assemblies of God.

In addition, the brethren from Springfield organized a duly authorized and approved District Council of the Assemblies of God organization. It consisted of Minnesota, Wisconsin, North and South Dakota, and Montana, and was called the North Central District Council of the Assemblies of God.

Rev. C.M. Hanson, fondly known as "Daddy Hanson," was appointed chairman, and Frank Lindquist was selected as vice-chairman. In about six months, Daddy Hanson resigned his position saying, "Give it to Frank Lindquist. He has a far better ability to do this work than I." So Frank Lindquist became the District Superintendent of the North Central District Council in June 1923, at the age of 24.

Later, under the leadership of Frank Lindquist, Lake Geneva Bible Camp was founded; this was the same camp where my father was healed and filled with the Holy Spirit, and where a young pastor by the name of O.W. Klingsheim felt called to start an Assemblies of God church in Paynesville, my hometown.

Many lives were touched by the Casino revival, both in 1922 and a later revival in the same church in 1938. Among the more prominent were Bartlett Peterson (a nephew of Ida and Axel Peterson's) who became a General Secretary for the Assemblies of God, and Andrew Hargrave, a local bartender who went on to attend North Central Bible Institute and later became a missionary to Brazil and Africa.

To this day, the small town of Casino has an Assemblies of God church, filled with warm, loving people. Marian and I were recently invited to help them celebrate their eightieth anniversary in their beautiful sanctuary that seats 400.

The results of the Casino revival spread far and wide, and affected many people, bringing them to God. But that revival did not begin on June 25th, 1922. Revival starts long before evidence can be seen, or manifestations felt. Revival often starts many, many years before any fruit is seen, and its roots are always in longing, and in sacrifice, and in prayer.

Move, and I Will Move

13

Facing Criticism

"My brothers, some from Chloe's household have informed me that there are quarrels among you."

1 Corinthians 1:11 (NIV)

"Make every effort to keep the unity of the Spirit through the bond of peace."

Ephesians 4:3 (NIV)

I hardly knew what to do. One of my congregation had turned against me.

The betrayal cut deeply. She was one of the original three ladies whose support had meant so much to me in that first cold winter in Little Falls. Her husband had joined the church and was now a board member. And yet for some reason, this woman began to gossip and speak critically of me.

What was at the root of this? Perhaps some hurt feelings, perhaps some minor disagreement—I didn't even know. But her criticisms were spreading throughout the congregation and the result was a growing discontent with, and distrust of, my leadership as pastor. Eventually the woman stopped attending church altogether.

I was only in my mid 20's. I was inexperienced and didn't know how to deal with this lady, but felt led not to confront her personally. Rather,

I spent much time in my office asking God to handle it for me.

There were several people that urged me to speak to her about her behavior, but as I prayed I felt a check in my spirit about confronting her. I felt God wanted me to stay in my place and continue praying. If I did that, He would bring the problem to my office.

One day her husband did indeed come to my office, asking why I had ignored his wife's absence.

I told him that I was deeply concerned about her, but that I was also more concerned about the things she had been spreading throughout the church. I answered that the Lord had led me to make it a matter of earnest prayer. Then I said, "I think you are the person that needs to confront your wife about the damage her criticism is doing in the church."

He said, "Pastor, I'll try."

Before he left I prayed for him, asking that God would give him the courage and the wisdom to handle the situation.

To my relief, within a few weeks this lady returned to church and became a staunch supporter of my leadership, and the dissension disappeared in the church.

I'm not recommending that others follow this manner of dealing with church difficulties unless they are led of God. God knows hearts and personalities. He can guide us in meeting and handling what may come.

Honest Questions over Spiritual Leadership

Every pastor has to deal with criticism. Sometimes there is a spirit of gossip, and the things at issue can be remarkably petty. But sometimes there is true doubt about the pastor's leadership in spiritual matters.

I faced this sort of criticism a few years later, during the Korean war.

Melvin Shadduck, a young man of our Little Falls congregation, was flying a plane on what was called a mosquito mission. This required flying just above the tree tops seeking to spot the enemy. When he did, he would drop flares so that our U.S. bombers would know where to drop their bombs.

Facing Criticism

One night his plane was shot down in enemy territory, and the Defense Department sent his parents, Lisle and Buela Shadduck, a notice that their son was missing in action.

That news was immediately aired by news reporter Cedric Adams on radio station WCCO. I rushed out to the Shadduck home to comfort them in this very dark hour.

As they were crying in pain and despair over this bad news, I discerned a spirit of gloom in the house. I began leading them in prayer. But as I prayed I suddenly experienced an inner glow.

It was so pronounced I knew it was God revealing to me that Melvin was still alive, and would be all right. After the 'Amen,' I told Melvin's parents what I had experienced while in prayer.

After a time, I returned to my office to pray. We had church the next morning, and I would have to announce the news. But how should I direct the congregation to pray?

If Melvin were truly alive, then our prayers should be for him, and his safe return. But if Melvin had been killed when his plane crashed, as most people thought, we wouldn't need to pray for him anymore, but rather should concentrate on praying that God would comfort his parents.

I had felt an inner glow, an assurance while praying at the Shadduck's home—but was that enough to justify a public assertion that everyone should keep praying for Melvin?

But as I was praying further in my office, God gave me a vision of Melvin standing in our Little Falls church, giving a testimony of how he had been rescued.

I had been given two strong assurances that Melvin was still alive! So the next morning, I announced

Facing the congregation at Little Falls

Move, and I Will Move

in church that we needed to pray earnestly for his rescue and safe return home.

However, virtually everyone assumed from the news release that he had been killed in the crash, and believed that this news would soon be reported. The people thought I was foolish to believe he was still alive. On the other hand, I really thought it would be foolish to pray for him if he were already dead.

The people began to takes sides on whether I should have taken the posture that Melvin was still alive. This was not so much in a spirit of gossip, but rather a concern that my spiritual direction wasn't the correct one, and would keep alive false hope, making things harder for the Shadduck family.

But God was gracious, and I continued to receive great assurance that Melvin was still alive, and in need of our prayers.

Two weeks later, I took Melvin's parents to a fellowship meeting in Brainerd. They had received no more news about their son and were terribly depressed. During the testimony service I sat on the platform and watched the Shadducks. They were in evident pain, and their faces clearly showed that they had no hope at all.

As I looked at them I prayed, "God, give Mr. Shadduck the faith to stand and give a testimony of faith that he believes Melvin is still alive, and that he will come home safely."

I had barely finished my prayer, when Lisle Shadduck stood to his feet, and with a note of faith in his voice said exactly what I had prayed for. Believe me, when I heard that, I felt like shouting! It gave me even more assurance to believe what God had shown me.

And the rest of the story? Well, Melvin was alive. He spent weeks behind enemy lines, surviving by eating vegetation. After many days he stumbled into a group of U.S. forces, and was taken to a hospital to recover from wounds received when his plane crashed.

Months later Melvin showed up for a Sunday service with his parents—and sat in the exact seat I had been shown in that vision.

Beaming, I asked, "Is there anyone who would like to give a testimony today?"

Immediately Melvin stood and testified to God's miraculous

intervention when he was shot down by the enemy in Korea. Our congregation erupted in praise to God. We, as a body of believers, became more convinced than ever before that God wants to answer the prayers of His people.

When Two Philosophies Clash

Sometimes a pastor is criticized because a member of the congregation has a fundamentally different way of looking at things. This may be because of personality, upbringing, or training—but a clash is inevitable, especially if the member is also on the board.

I once had a board member who was brought up in poverty by a fiscally conservative dad, and had inherited the same philosophy of penny pinching. So it wasn't hard to understand why he always tried to block attempts by the board to be generous in their money decisions.

This conservative attitude became a huge challenge to me. I wanted to develop our people into a congregation of generous givers, but this man continued to frustrate my efforts.

One day as I was praying about the matter, I felt the Lord lead me to confront him privately. So, as Ephesians 4:15 directs, I determined to speak the truth in love.

As I met with him I said, "Dick, weren't you brought up by parents who were extremely conservative, financially?"

He answered, "Yes, that's true."

I told him that I was raised by a father who was always generous, and gave freely. As a result, I had developed his same philosophy. I told Dick that through the years God had blessed my positive and generous attitude, and that was the philosophy I wanted this church to adopt.

"God has positioned me as leader of this church," I said, "and I appeal to you to adopt this same philosophy for your own benefit, and also for the benefit of our church." And I finished with a quotation of the Apostle Paul's in 2 Corinthians 9:6-7:

"But this I say: he who sows sparingly will also reap sparingly, and he who sows bountifully will also reap bountifully. So let each one give as he purposes in his heart, not grudgingly or of necessity; for God loves a cheerful giver."

Dick said, "Pastor, I see your point, and I'll try to submit to your leadership."

I'm sure it was the Holy Spirit that caused him to see the light. From that day forward, Dick manifested a different attitude toward the Lord's work. He developed into a very generous person and is a great blessing to the work of the Lord to this day. The congregation has also matured, becoming a very generous people who look for opportunities to give and bless those at home and around the world.

Dealing With a Divisive Spirit

Criticism can come in many forms, and for many reasons. But it is most destructive when a person intends to sow division, with the ultimate goal of taking control. This is an assault on the spiritual authority of the pastor, and is devastating for the church.

I once had a board member whose words were music to my ears. He was an influential man in the church, and one of my strongest supporters. But one day I found it necessary to support the discipline of a member of his family.

This board member was furious, and turned on me. He absolutely could not believe his family member had committed the act which got him into trouble with the law and the church, in spite of all the evidence to the contrary.

I counseled privately with my friend, and the two of us prayed together. I thought the problem had been solved between us. However, when he went home and shared our conversation with his wife, she convinced him that I was wrong, and that their family member wasn't guilty.

The family member in question was eventually convicted by the courts and sentenced. But that didn't settle it for the board member.

His words that once had been music to my ears now became daggers in my heart. A divisive spirit began to rear its ugly head as this man met with the members of our church in small groups before and after every service. He was using all his influence to sow discord, in an attempt to win support for his point of view.

A few of the people he talked to reported the dissension and divisive talk to me. I was told that he had said, "I can outlast Arvid." To my deep dismay, it became clear that he was determined to divide the congregation.

Facing Criticism

The situation made for a lot of pressure, and I didn't have a clue what my response should be. But somehow I felt that as pastor of hundreds of people it was my responsibility to deal with the situation.

We had a little cabin in the woods about 90 miles from home, so I decided to go and spend time praying for guidance. I always pray best in the woods!

When I arrived at the cabin, it was raining so heavily that I was tempted to stay inside, but I took an umbrella and went out anyway, praying and seeking the Lord for guidance.

Soon the rain became so heavy that I stopped under a huge tree for shelter. The sadness I was feeling over this situation, and what it was doing to our church, overwhelmed me. The umbrella I was carrying kept me dry, but my tears made my face very wet.

Standing there crying, groaning, interceding, I suddenly heard God's inaudible voice inside my being saying just five words taken from Matthew 16:18: *"I WILL BUILD MY CHURCH."* At that moment it dawned on me that the church I was so concerned about building wasn't my responsibility, but His! Suddenly, relief flooded my spirit, and the pressure I had been experiencing disappeared. I began to praise the Lord that He had taken the responsibility to build Bloomington Assembly of God Church, and joy crowded out all my grief.

At the next board meeting this man was present. I have never been a fan of confrontation, but I had a new freedom in my spirit to follow the direction found in the eighteenth chapter of Matthew.

I described to the other board members what had been taking place. I told this man directly that if he did not stop his divisiveness in the congregation, he should resign from the board and leave the church. He eventually left, and in time the ugly wound healed.

Since the day God spoke to me in the woods and said: "I will build My church," I've had great peace working for Him. The rest of that verse assured me that I never again needed to worry about problems in the church because, as Matthew 16:18 says, *"the gates of Hell shall not prevail against it"* (KJV).

In the course of time, anyone who pastors discovers that people problems arise. There will be gossip, and doubt. There will be differences of opinion and philosophy. And there may even be someone who is bent on division and control.

But when we turn to God's word, we discover in Proverbs 6:19 that *"the Lord hates... one who sows discord among the brethren."* He truly knows how to handle any situation given to Him.

14

Work and Lots Of It

"We did not act in an undisciplined manner among you, nor did we eat anyone's bread without paying for it, but with labor and hardship we kept working night and day..."
2 Thessalonians 3:7b-8a (NASB)

I sat at the kitchen table in the old farmhouse, absolutely overwhelmed. I was fourteen years old, and I was facing a task I wasn't sure I could handle.

Oh, I had been cocky enough the night before—even magnanimous. Bible camp was in session at Lake Geneva and I had said to my family, "Why don't you all go. I'll handle the chores."

Grateful for the offer, they had left me in charge of the farm. I was the man of the place now; I could hardly wait to get going, and prove I could do it all. So I got up early and began with the milking.

We had no milking machines. I don't think I can quite convey to you what it means to milk forty head of cattle by hand. My hands were so tired, I could scarcely finish the last few cows. After that, I filled their feedboxes, then fed the sheep, threw hay to the horses, fed the chickens, and slopped the pigs. By the time I went in to have a little breakfast, it was almost lunchtime. I had something to eat, then looked at the clock—and groaned. It was almost time to start milking again, given how long I knew it was going to take me. After that, I would have to feed all the animals once more—and there were other chores too, such as carrying water for the animals, and tossing hay down from the barn.

That's when I put my head in my hands, sure I had bitten off more than I could chew. But there wasn't anything else to be done—I had to get back to work, because those animals were depending on me, and there was no one else to do it.

It was very late when I finished milking. After all the remaining chores were done, I went in to have a long overdue supper. And as I tumbled into bed, weary beyond belief, I vowed, "Never again. I will *never* do this again."

But, of course, I did.

For although I never repeated that particular mistake on the farm, my basic personality didn't change. As an adult, I still had an inner drive to do more and do it better, to step up to the challenge and prove I could handle extra responsibility. When I became a pastor, that meant I got a lot accomplished—but I also paid a price, and often a price that I hadn't anticipated.

The Workload Increases

By 1950 in Little Falls, my life was very full. Marian and I now had two young children—Kathy, age three, and Doug, a baby. We had been several years in our new building with its educational wing and were meeting the mortgage payments; attendance was about 125 weekly, and growing steadily.

I had been elected a presbyter of the East Central Section, and I was still state D-Cap, president of the Christ's Ambassadors youth program for the district. By this time, I was running several youth camps a summer, rallies throughout the state during the rest of the year, and doing follow-up with pastors to help support their youth programs. Except for a nagging case of eczema which would come on every summer near the end of the youth camps, I was happy in my work and handling the load. But my mentor, Ivan O. Miller, had even more in mind.

Besides my parents, the one person that influenced my ministry the most was Ivan O. Miller. He had been my professor of pastoral theology

Work and Lots Of It

at North Central, and a great inspiration. And he was the one who had asked me to consider leaving a position as assistant pastor in Sioux City, Iowa, to pioneer a church in Little Falls.

But now he was calling me again, and his invitation was urgent. Fall semester had just begun at North Central and the director of the music department had suddenly resigned. Would I consider taking the position? "We really need you right away, Arvid!"

I didn't want to leave Little Falls—and certainly not so suddenly. I was still their pastor, after all! But Brother Miller said, "You can do both jobs, Arvid. Just give us two days a week."

I thought I could manage the commute, but I was not at all certain of my ability to handle the position. While I had led singing, played trombone, traveled in a quartet and directed a youth choir in the years since graduation, I knew that some of the choir and orchestra members at North Central would be trained musicians. How could I lead them? I would have to undertake further musical training at the very least, I decided.

I prayed about the matter, and felt a nudge of the Spirit to accept the offer. I told my church board about it, and they seemed satisfied that I would still be able to continue as pastor for most of the time.

So twice a week I caught a train at 4:00 a.m. in Little Falls, and took a street car from the Great Northern Depot in Minneapolis to NCBI in time for classes. Later in the afternoon I walked to MacPhail School of Music to attend classes myself, and then took a train back home in the evenings. Those two days turned out to be very difficult for me physically and emotionally, but I was determined to follow through on my commitment.

The next summer, I ran the usual youth camps and developed my usual case of eczema, a dry and itching skin condition that, once the camps closed, generally took about six weeks to go away. But this time, the eczema never cleared up. And for the whole school year following, Marian and I both experienced a restlessness of the spirit, a sort of flightiness, and a sense that there was something else ahead.

We found out what it was in June of 1952 when Ivan O. Miller called with a new offer. He wanted me at NCBI full time—to teach Bible classes, to continue as director of the music department, and to take on the position of director of public relations, which would involve a fair amount of travel. Of course this would mean resigning from the church in Little Falls—and it was a difficult decision. I had thoroughly enjoyed building a congregation, and really didn't want to leave. At that point we had about 200 who came regularly, with perhaps 140 attending on any given Sunday.

Shortly after, at our annual Sunday School picnic, I sat on a table at Lindbergh Park with Sunday School Superintendent Bud Norwood, who had become a very personal friend. Our companionship had deepened through times of hunting and fishing together, and so I told him about North Central's invitation and my struggle to leave. I felt that I was letting him down as a friend.

He said, "Arvid, we certainly don't want you to leave us, but if that's what the Lord wants, you'd better accept."

I still wasn't sure, so I put a fleece before the Lord that week. I said to the Lord, "If you want me to leave Little Falls, then give me a sign. Have someone come forward next Sunday morning for salvation."

No one had come forward for this purpose for some time. But that next Sunday, after giving the altar call, I raised my head after prayer—and saw through my tears that one person had come forward.

It was my own little daughter, Kathy.

My brother, Delmar, became available and accepted the Little Falls invitation to become their second pastor. This helped ease the move for me and the church, so I resigned with a light heart and accepted the invitation to join North Central's faculty full time.

Full Time at North Central

Marian and I borrowed money from both sets of parents for a down payment on a house in the cities. We didn't have much furniture, so packing wasn't difficult. I got Marian and the children settled in a house in St. Louis Park, left her with the car (now very old and unreliable, with bad tires), and promptly took off for a summer of traveling, doing student procurement for NCBI and raising funds for the school from alumni. I did a lot of hitchhiking to get where I needed to go!

That summer, although I had given up the position of state D-Cap, and knew I would no longer have to run the stress-producing youth camps, my eczema continued to bother me. Still, I was enjoying my work. Ivan O. Miller would write letters of introduction to the district superintendents of the areas I planned to visit, and send materials ahead so they would be waiting for me when I got to town. I would set up a table display at a church or camp meeting, talk to potential students, and answer questions.

One of the first places I went to that summer was a camp meeting in Wisconsin. A young man came up and asked some questions, and I tried to give him a brochure. He waved it away and said, "Aah, give it to somebody else."

I said, "You just take it, and pray about it." And the next morning that same man came back with the brochure, filled in with his registration information. His name was Monroe Grams—a man who not only went to North Central, but later became a missionary to South America!

In the fall I was back at NCBI, feeling my way into the new full time position.

I was working very hard, anxious to do well, but we had taken a pay cut to come to NCBI, and were making payments on a house as well. Marian played the piano for the Minneapolis Gospel Tabernacle, Frank J. Lindquist's church, for $30 a month—and I traveled many Sundays, speaking at various churches as a supply, or substitute, pastor. Money was so tight that any money I got from speaking went straight for groceries.

I must say that it was hard for me to go into a church, give one sermon, and then leave. As a boy on the farm, I had not only planted seed, but I had also watered and weeded and watched it grow to maturity. As a pastor, I wanted to stick around for the whole process, too. For me, it was terribly unsatisfying to speak the word of God, and never see the results in people's lives.

I was learning a lot, though. For one thing, teaching Bible classes meant that I really dug into the scriptures, reading many commentaries and doing research that I had never done as either a college student or a pastor. I learned more about the Bible as a teacher than I ever had as a student—and I had the practical application to offer as well, having been a pastor for so many years.

I had been given yet another responsibility at NCBI—that of the Christian Service Department, which entailed assigning students to various Twin Cities churches to do ministry. So my own students were getting opportunities for ministry in one church—something I was beginning to crave.

The Birth of Bloomington Assembly of God

And then in January, 1953, there was a new opportunity for me; and once again it came from Ivan O. Miller. He called me into his office and said, "Arvid, several of our children are living in the city of Bloomington and I'm concerned that there's no Assemblies of God church there. Do you think you could get one started through the Christian Service Department?" I said: "I'll pray about it, and let you know."

I got right into my car and drove south to Bloomington. I had no idea where to go, but I was looking for any building in which we could conduct services. All of a sudden I came upon an old school house that was padlocked.

I walked to a neighbor's house and asked a man what he knew about the place. He said that it belonged to the Bloomington School District, and I should contact Hubert Olson, who was the superintendent of the Bloomington schools. Immediately I went to see Mr. Olson and told him of my intent to find a building in which to start a church.

"Is that school building at 86th and Cedar for sale?" I asked.

"Well, it could be," he said. "We're having a school board meeting this week and I'll make it an agenda item, and I'll let you know what we decide." In a few days I received a call from Mr. Olson stating the Board had decided to sell the old Kimball school on sealed bids.

I contacted the Minneapolis Savings and Loan and asked for an appraiser. He met me at the site and said, "Our bank will loan you $15,000 on this property." I then talked with two of the men that had an interest in an Assemblies of God church beginning in Bloomington. They suggested we submit a bid a little higher than the appraised value because other interested bidders might also have it appraised.

Work and Lots Of It

So we submitted a bid for $15,313.00. We didn't have the additional $313.00, but we felt that if God wanted us to have the building, He'd provide. Well, God must have wanted us to have it because our bid was accepted!

We borrowed the $15,000, and took an offering from interested friends for the $313. And then we went to work to clean up the old school house.

It was a two room schoolhouse, so we removed the center partition, making it into a single room suitable for worship services. We needed to add partitions in the basement for Sunday School rooms, though. Curt Carlson, one of our original members and an employee of Chrysler, had a good idea.

The old Kimball Schoolhouse became Bloomington Assembly of God Church

The Packard car company had gone out of business, and he thought we could get some of their upholstery material for little or nothing. He brought it in on big bolts eight feet high! We cut the fabric in 25-foot sections and strung wire to hang the curtains, and in this way we made about a dozen rooms for Sunday School.

Curt was an original member in more than one sense, for when he was a boy he had attended the Kimball School, and had even swung on the rope to ring the school bell that we now used to announce Sunday service. (Within a few years I would dedicate his baby son Rod, who grew up to become the senior pastor of Oak Hills Church in Eagan, a daughter church of Bloomington Assembly.)

We scrubbed the cement schoolhouse floor, and then we painted it. We washed windows and we set up chairs. It took a good many days and much hard labor to prepare the building for services, but at last we held the first service on Sunday, March 3, 1953.

Rev. Ivan O. Miller gave the message. The North Central choral group which I had been conducting, the Evangelaires, provided the music. Incidentally, one of the altos in that choir was Lou Crawford, who, with her husband Bob, are long term faithful members of this church. Our attendance at that first service, not counting the choir, was 27 people—including babies!

We Ask For Two Signs

This was an exciting time for me, but it was also a very difficult and uncertain time. I was working hard to get the church building in good shape, and had taken on the self-appointed role of pastor to these 27 people. I preached at Bloomington on Sundays, but I was not yet the official pastor, for the church had not yet been organized or held an election.

Someone else could still come in and replace me, if that was what the people wished, or if Ivan O. Miller decided someone else would be better in the position. I very much wanted to be pastor of a church again—I missed it terribly—and yet there were obstacles.

One was the lack of a reliable car, with good tires. If I became the pastor of the Bloomington church, there would be many trips back and forth. Hitchhiking was not a realistic option in this situation!

Another problem was that my eczema, an indicator of stress for me, had become severe. In addition to all my other North Central duties, I had just been given responsibility for running the graduation ceremonies in June. I had taken on the pastorship of a new church, as well as janitorial and handyman roles, but it was by no means certain that I would be the permanent pastor.

Marian was still bringing the children to Sunday School at the Gospel Tabernacle and playing there for the choir. She didn't want to give up a paying job to come and play the piano at the little Bloomington church unless she knew I was going to be the pastor for sure, but I missed her terribly. I longed for us to be working together in ministry, building a church, as we had done before in Little Falls.

The uncertainty, the workload, and the fact that Marian and I hadn't been able to work together in ministry for so long, combined to create a monster of a skin condition for me. The eczema that had troubled me for almost two years now moved into my scalp and into the skin around and inside my eyes. At night, I would scratch in my sleep—and in the morning would wake up with my scalp pitted with gouges, and with blood running from my eyes. Nothing we tried had helped, including prayer.

Unbeknownst to me, Marian put out a fleece to God, and said that if it was His will that I become the pastor at Bloomington Assembly, she would know it because we would have an additional $1,000—the figure she thought we needed in order to swing the added expense of a better car, and the extra gas mileage costs.

And unbeknownst to Marian, I also put out a fleece, saying that if my eczema cleared up, I would consider it a sign that it was God's will that I become pastor at Bloomington.

And God Adds a Miracle!

About this time, I was working with two other men on the exterior of the school building, scraping the peeling paint. We were standing on ladders, with a blow torch in one hand and a scraper in the other. The man next to me was working on a window frame. He softened paint with his blow torch, and then held it away while he scraped the softened paint away. He was not aware that when he held his blow torch away the torch was shooting fire into a mouse hole and sending flames into the dry walls of the old building.

All at once I heard the roar of the spreading fire and saw smoke coming from various parts of the building. I hurried down my ladder, ran around the building to where the third man was working, told him what was happening, then ran into the building and climbed the belfry ladder to see if the fire had reached into the attic.

To this day I'm wondering about the wisdom of that. As I reached the attic I could hear the fire roaring louder and louder, and I began to panic. In my moment of hopeless desperation I cried out with a loud voice, "FIRE, STOP!"

At that moment I heard a fire truck's siren as it approached the school. A neighbor had seen the smoke and called the fire department. Knowing that I needed to hurry out of that attic, I quickly climbed down the belfry ladder to find a fireman tearing out a board from the wall where the fire had started.

As I looked at the board, I saw charred wood where the flames had eaten into it. But there was no fire. The roaring had ceased.

The men from the fire department asked, "Where's the fire?" They were dumbfounded; the old schoolhouse was all wood, and dry as tinder. But God had put out the fire, so they put their water hoses back on their truck and left.

What a miracle, and what a great encouragement to me—and it was a sign from God that I hadn't even asked for!

Adding to the encouragement, Marian had seen an advertisement for a soothing soap and salve that was supposed to help dry and itching skin. She got it, and it turned out to help my eczema as nothing else had done.

And then one day we opened a letter from my parents, in which my father wrote that he was forgiving $1,000 worth of our debt to him—a portion of the money we owed him for the down payment of our house, which we had been repaying with interest at the rate of $50 a month.

It seemed that God really was calling me to pastor the fledgling church; and in June of 1953, the little congregation called me, too. G. Raymond Carlson came to preside over the organization of the church; the constitution and bylaws were accepted, and I was voted in as permanent pastor of Bloomington Assembly of God. My salary was $25 a week.

I'm in my eighties now, and I've slowed down some. Yet my son Doug said just the other day, "Dad has one setting—*GO*." I guess I haven't changed all that much. And, looking back, it does seem as if I took on far more than I should have. I paid a price, and my family got less of my time than they would have liked.

But taking on such a workload, with so many varied duties, helped me in one way. My tenure at North Central helped me learn to organize my time very well, and honed my administrative abilities—skills that I would need as the Bloomington church grew.

And one more thing became very clear during this time in my life. I knew that I would have to set some boundaries.

I had to learn to take care of myself, I had to allow more time for family, I had to learn to say "No" on occasion—and I had to learn to delegate.

15

Giving Up Control

"These twelve Jesus sent out after instructing them..."
Matthew 10:5a (NASB)

The bike was new, shiny, and my little daughter Kathy wanted to ride it.

She had every right to ride it. It was a gift from her grandfather on her fifth birthday. But she needed my help to learn. So I ran alongside, hanging on for dear life, coaching her with every turn of the pedals.

The pastor of a small church is like that. At first he oversees everything, holding on tightly and coaching people constantly.

When my church was small I attended every function, supervised every soloist and ensemble, went to every open house and every graduation. I visited my parishioners in their homes, and ate dinner with them as well. I had a personal relationship with every one of my congregation, and I was their shepherd.

As long as the church is small, this kind of supervision is fine. In fact, it's a boon to the young pastor. Having a finger in every pot, and having responsibility for the whole, gives him a priceless chance to sharpen his talents. He grows along with his church, and begins to learn how to handle any number of situations with grace and maturity.

God loves small churches. Jesus let us know that in no uncertain terms when He said in Matthew 18:20, "where two or three are gathered together in my name, I am there in the midst of them."

It's a good thing, too, for over 80% of the churches in the United States have fewer than 100 members! Jesus doesn't differentiate between small or large gatherings of people. He manifests His presence whenever or wherever people gather in His name.

We read in Acts 19:7 that the apostle Paul visited the church in Ephesus which had only twelve members. Verse six says that when he laid his hands on them, the Holy Spirit came upon them, and they spoke with tongues and prophesied. A study of church history and the whole Pentecostal movement is filled with examples of God manifesting His presence to small gatherings of believers.

So there is nothing wrong with pastoring a small church!

But as your church starts to grow—and God loves growing churches—you will find that you must learn to let go. You have to give other people a chance to find their balance, test their skills, and ride the bike on their own.

When I was teaching my daughter Kathy to ride her bike, there came a moment when she was pedaling so fast I could barely keep up. She was achieving a sort of balance, and I was getting tired—and so I let go.

She wobbled precariously. My heart skipped a beat or two. But she triumphed, riding away from me with a glowing face. Kathy had become, in those few short moments, a little less dependent on me. She had grown.

But just consider how awful it would have been if I had never brought myself to let go of Kathy. I might have said to myself, "She'll wobble. She might fall. It'll be safer if I just keep hanging on."

Some pastors are like that with their churches. They are not able to give up on the perfectionism. They know that if they delegate some tasks, the job won't be done as well at first. So some guys just don't give it up. The result? Burnout for them—and a church that never really grows up.

Beginning to Delegate

In the early years of my ministry I made it a must-do to visit people in their homes during the week that they first visited our church. I got

Giving Up Control

acquainted with their children, and always prayed with the family before I left.

When the church membership reached 100, and I knew I needed help to survive the demands of ministry, I didn't choose to delegate the visiting portion. In my judgment, visiting people in their own homes was the reason for much of the numerical growth of our church. Since I was still the only paid person on staff, I had to delegate various other responsibilities to members of my congregation.

When you begin to delegate, at first it will be with volunteers, and then with part time staff. An important piece of delegating is to resist the temptation to take the job back, once you have given it.

Expect that the person learning a new skill will wobble a bit. Expect that the job won't be done as well as you would have done it, or in the same style. But also expect to see a great deal of growth—and remember that just as God blessed your early attempts, and kindly forgave your blunders, you should return the favor!

Incidentally, I noticed that those who assumed responsibility experienced much faster spiritual growth in their lives than those who were just church attendees. Furthermore, they were the happiest people because it gave them the joy of being active contributors to the kingdom of God.

As I released others to help carry the load, they came through for me. Delegating allowed others to share more fully in ministry. That's a win-win situation.

Family Matters

Delegating some of the work will give you more time for your family, too. The balancing act between work and family is difficult for every parent, but can be especially challenging for a pastor, who sometimes feels as if he must choose between his children and God.

When I was a boy, I spent a lot of time with my dad simply because we lived on a farm. Dad would work right alongside of us boys, teaching us the best way to do things, and there was a lot of companionship in that.

But when my generation began to move off the farm and take jobs in the cities, we weren't able to spend our working hours with our children. Family time had to be scheduled, and unfortunately for my children, many of my pastoral obligations were in the evenings and on weekends.

It is worth remembering that, while church matters can be delegated to others, our children cannot. Looking back, there are some special things I missed that I wish I hadn't.

My daughter Kathy played the piano and violin, and by junior high was developing at a rapid rate musically. But many of her concerts were on Sunday afternoons—a difficult time for a pastor who has to preach twice in the morning and give a new sermon in the evening. I had to miss some of her concerts, to my sorrow.

One thing I *was* able to do, though, was to take her to her rehearsals with the youth symphony. I'd sit in the back and listen to her practice. In this way, I got to hear a concert almost every week!

As she grew older, I got to hear her more because she played for the choir at church. Musically, she was a natural, and I was just so proud of how well she could play. But more than that; I found that now *she* was the one ministering to me, through her music. And in the years since that time, as I have watched her use her musical gifts in ministry, I've been so glad that we were able to give her the lessons she needed to nurture her talent, and that I'd been able to carve out the time to support her even though I hadn't been at every concert.

Kathy remembers one time, though, when I was scheduled to attend a concert of hers. She was going to play a tympani solo, and she was very excited that I was coming to hear her. But at the last minute, I was called in to an emergency meeting. Whether it related to the church, or to my North Central Bible College or presbyter responsibilities, I don't recall. But when I broke the news to her in the car, as I drove her to the rehearsal prior to the concert, she began to cry.

Kathy tells me that I *did* attend her concert that night. And although I don't remember now how many calls I had to make to get out of the meeting, and I am sure the people at the meeting have long forgotten that I didn't attend, my daughter remembers to this day that I was there for her. I am thankful that, once in a while, I got it right!

Giving Up Control

Conflicts between work and family were sometimes made more complicated by my own conscience, and the attitudes of those influential in my life.

My son Douglas played three sports a year. I was able to attend many more of his games than Kathy's concerts because there were more of them, and they weren't on Sundays (at least not until he was grown and playing for the Vikings). Still, I often had a conflict with my work schedule.

I had been raised in a church where the pastor preached against sports, especially if they interfered with church activities. If someone chose a sporting event over something that was scheduled at the church, it was considered an affront to God.

I felt less guilty about my love of sports, though, the day I saw this very pastor pull up to a cabin at Lake Geneva, and open the trunk of his car. It was packed with sports equipment! He had teenagers of his own by that time, and his thinking had undergone a change. I began to see that perhaps it wasn't as necessary to stay away from sports as I had been told.

But I still wrestled with this regarding Doug. I loved watching him play, yet I couldn't feel easy in my conscience if I put his games ahead of anything related to the church. I missed two very special games of his because of Wednesday night prayer meeting and a responsibility at North Central Bible College, and I regret it to this day.

The year Doug was in ninth grade, he began to get a lot of attention for his athletic ability. His coaches were talking to me, letting me know that he had great potential for landing college scholarships, and even playing professionally someday. And it was just at this time that Thomas Zimmerman, the general superintendent for the Assemblies of God, called me with an offer.

"The General Council Committee unanimously elected you, Arvid," he said. "We want you to take the post of Home Missions Director. It's a national position, though, and you'd need to move to headquarters."

I was flattered to be asked, and the job appealed to me. But how would a move affect the children?

By this time, Kathy was almost ready for college; she would be leaving the nest soon in any case. And Lynne and Boni, our two youngest, were eight and two years old—young enough to relocate without much trouble. But Doug was another story. He was strongly coming into the limelight, and taking a leadership role on his teams. If I moved the family to Springfield, Missouri, he'd be terribly unhappy. He'd have to start all over again in a new place, and it would undoubtedly hurt his future in the sports he loved so much.

Well, I laid it before the Lord. And the verse that gradually came to the fore in my mind was this: *"But if anyone does not provide for his own, and especially for those of his household, he has denied the faith, and is worse than an unbeliever"* (1 Timothy 5:8).

It became clear to me that this wasn't a choice between God and sports—this was about building my career at the expense of my son. I chose to stay where I was.

And, unlike those special games I missed, this is one choice I have never regretted.

Hiring Staff: Ego Issues

Delegating some of the work to volunteers will work well for a time. But as your church grows you will need to hire staff to help you.

There is a big threshold when your church reaches 250 or so. As a pastor, you will find that you can no longer have a personal relationship with each member of your congregation.

They will still call you in a crisis, and want a hospital visit; but at this point, certain people who like the personal relationship with the head guy will go to another church. They will say, "This church is too big for us."

I tried to hire a full time staff member

1964: Bloomington Assembly of God Church at 94th and Portland. This was the first section built. Later, we added a sanctuary, and this portion became the Fellowship Hall.

Giving Up Control

for every 150 people, and I found that the new people didn't just help me share the load of ministry, but they also broadened my base, so to speak. Each new staff person brought new skills and ministries to the table. They had abilities that I did not have.

A successful pastor ideally finds out what he is good at; then he hires staff around those strengths, in order to fill in for his own weaknesses. But this is also where some pastors fall down.

When you begin to hire staff, you find out pretty quickly what portion of your satisfaction in your work comes from seeing the kingdom of God enlarged, and what part comes from ego. When you see people you have hired doing better at a job than you did, you have to be excited about that, not resentful. You have to let them run with the job, the requirements, and their God given abilities.

Some pastors can't do this. They hire someone to help them, and then when they notice that the person hired is actually doing a wonderful job—better than the senior pastor did—and people are responding to the new person in ways that the senior pastor couldn't elicit, the senior pastor might actually begin to sabotage that new hire in subtle ways.

This type of pastor just can't let go of being the main contact for the people in his congregation. He gets jealous, and the work suffers. Gradually there gets to be a spirit of divisiveness and pettiness, and the people under him are restless and constrained. The ministry becomes more about the senior pastor's ego, and how people relate to him and his authority, rather than about the work of the kingdom of God.

The senior pastor *cannot* be jealous of those under him. He must be willing to let junior staff have the main contact with people in the congregation. He must be willing to let junior staff preach now and then, and to rejoice in their successes.

Can They Deliver?

When seeking to fill a staff position, there are certain qualities to look for that guarantee the candidate will be a good choice over the long haul.

Obviously, you will need to find a person qualified and trained for the particular job which needs to be done. For example, if you are looking for a children's pastor you wouldn't think of hiring a person whose strengths are in the field of senior adults. That would be like trying to fit a square peg into a round hole. If you're looking for a minister of music, you would take great pains to find a person who has had experience in that field, and has a particular gifting in the ministry of music.

But training and skills in their particular area of ministry is not enough.

I once had a minister of music who had been adequately trained musically, and had a vision of what he wanted music to accomplish in the church, but couldn't figure out the steps needed to be taken to accomplish that vision. He'd announce a goal for the choir and orchestra which got everybody excited, but he didn't have a clue what it would take to reach that goal. Consequently, he became frustrated, the musicians became discouraged, and I found it necessary to let him go.

In retrospect, my mistake was not in firing him, but in not doing a more through job of evaluating his abilities before I did the hiring.

Since that unfortunate experience, I have been looking not only for self starters—but also self finishers! I need people who know how to get the job done. I'm also concerned if they know how to delegate, or if they are micro-managers. Someone who cannot give up control is someone who will get in the way of growth.

Character Issues

Some character issues are obvious red flags; sexual misconduct springs to mind, as well as any kind of dishonesty. But there are also more subtle character flaws that, while they may not seem as large at first, will cause great trouble among your staff and within the church.

Some years ago I needed a youth pastor, so I put up my antenna to locate a good one. There were numerous inexperienced ones fresh out of college available, but I felt a large church needed someone with considerable experience, so I phoned a successful youth evangelist on the west coast for recommendations.

I knew that this evangelist had been traveling the length and breadth of the United States conducting youth revival campaigns, and thought that certainly he would be able to recommend someone who was doing a good job as a youth pastor. He came up with the name of a fellow in Texas, and gave him a strong recommendation.

I called this young man, and talked at length with him about what he had accomplished and was currently doing. He impressed me on the phone, and I said I might be calling him again about the possibility of coming to the Twin Cities to look our situation over. He said he was open to such an invitation.

I then called the church this man was working in and spoke to the secretary. I told her what I was doing, and she suggested that I talk to the pastor.

She put him on the line; I said his youth pastor had been highly recommended to me. The pastor encouraged me to proceed. He said that his youth pastor had done a good job, but that he was thinking about making a change.

Then I called the young man's presbyter and asked if he would recommend the guy, and the presbyter gave a good report—except he had a reservation on one point.

Right away that sent up a red flag for me. I called the man's pastor again, and asked about the point the presbyter had mentioned. The pastor said, "Well, since you brought it up, there is an issue there."

The problem was simply that this man would go ahead and do things without permission.

This could seem like a simple lack of experience. After all, don't senior pastors want people under them to be self starters? No boss wants to hand hold all the time—he expects people to know their job and do it, right? Perhaps this young man just didn't know where the line was.

Every new hire has to figure this out for himself. The line between being timid and not having enough initiative, and being overbearing and having too much, is different with every new boss and every new church.

But in this man's case, the underlying issue was one of character; and this became clear in his reaction to correction. When he was told that he had overstepped his bounds, he did not pull back and adjust his style. Instead, he asserted his right to control his area, without consulting with anyone. And as a result of his arrogance, he made some poor decisions that ended up causing conflict, not only with the senior pastor and staff, but also among the congregation.

This man had impressed the evangelist whose opinion I had sought, because he was a smart guy with energy. But the evangelist had not had to work with him on a daily basis, or deal with this young man's abrasive insensitivity to others, and unwillingness to learn or subject himself to authority.

Maybe the young man in question would learn in time. Maybe the conflict he was experiencing in his current position would make him more teachable in his next.

Maybe—but I didn't want to be the guinea pig. My bet was that the reason the senior pastor had given this young man such a strong recommendation was because he hoped I'd hire the guy, and that would be an easy way to say goodbye. Needless to say, I quickly crossed that name off the list.

Another character issue is diligence—or the lack thereof. Laziness shows itself in many ways, and is always off-putting.

I once had a fellow on my staff who lived near the church. He'd come racing over just in the nick of time as service began, and arrive at his chair on the platform barely put together. He wouldn't even have brushed his teeth, and his breath would almost knock me over. This is pretty bad if you're going to pray with people!

Sometimes lazy habits are the result of youth. A young man often has no idea how he comes across to others. His parents probably tried to train him, but the young man may have decided their lessons weren't important.

He might grow out of it eventually, but in the meantime he is not impressing his boss or the people who have to work with him. After awhile, people get tired of covering for him and making excuses for his lapses.

If he doesn't correct himself, lazy habits become ingrained character flaws, and work against him all his life. Proverbs 13:4 says: *"The soul of a sluggard desires, and has nothing; but the soul of the diligent shall be made rich."*

Nothing is more demoralizing than empty dreams and shattered hopes, but this is the inevitable portion of the lazy person. On the other hand, when a person applies the qualities of diligence to all his living and serving, there will be richness of soul—and the result is both dedication and satisfaction. The person that is not only a self starter, but also a self finisher is imbued with a passion that has the power to make things happen!

Two other characteristics are important to examine: namely, loyalty and trust. These must be absolutes.

The scriptures say, "Trust in the Lord with all your heart." The verb literally means "to cling to"; yes, with both arms! Along the Christian pathway, Jesus must have all of us; a handshake is not enough. He wants us to trust Him, and He wants our loyalty.

The scriptures don't say, "Trust in your senior pastor with all your heart," but sometimes I wished I could have quoted a verse like that. A senior pastor is not just a boss; he is also a shepherd, responsible for those given into his keeping. As such, his primary care is for souls, and doing whatever it takes to guide and guard them—and he has been given authority, by God and by the church leadership, for this task.

There are enough challenges in this assignment, without the added stress of under-shepherds that decide it's not important to follow their leader. The sheep get confused, the work suffers, and the senior pastor either gets an ulcer, or fires the guy.

Disagreements can be aired, and differences of opinion can be talked over; but ultimately, if someone on staff can't go along with the senior pastor's guidelines, then that person should be honest about it and seek employment elsewhere.

A staff member who knows the senior pastor's wishes, but does something else behind the pastor's back, is disloyal. If a junior staffer can't trust the pastor enough to accept his leading, whether the matter is large or small, then how can the senior pastor give trust in return?

The staff member who refuses to follow the senior pastor is undermining the leader who was set above him, and whose authority he accepted when he took the job. This is not scriptural, as Hebrews 13:17 makes plain: *"Obey your leaders, and submit to them; for they keep watch over your souls, as those who will give an account. Let them do this with joy and not*

Move, and I Will Move

with grief, for this would be unprofitable for you." (NASB)

Of course I am not talking about a situation where a senior pastor has broken God's laws, and is in moral failure. I would not expect staff to blindly follow, or to cover the tracks of the senior pastor's sinful behavior.

But as a general rule, a pastor, to be effective in his work, needs people around him that he can trust. He needs staff who remain loyal to him and to the standards that he sets, or he cannot delegate with any confidence.

More Growth Means More Delegation

By the time the church I started in Bloomington reached 500 people attending on Sunday mornings, my paid staff consisted of a church secretary, a Christian education director, a minister of music, a youth pastor, and janitors. Having all these staff members didn't lighten my load as senior pastor. It did help our church to better serve the various needs of the growing congregation.

I found myself increasingly frustrated that I couldn't seem to catch up on any front. I knew I needed to spend more time in prayer and study if I was to be any kind of pastor at all. I wanted to be more available to my family, especially to Lynne and Boni who were still at home; and I wanted to do God's work in the church. But there was so much of it!

One day when I was lying on the prayer room floor agonizing before God that I had altogether too much work to do, He spoke to me, saying: "Why don't you share the work of the church with the people of the church?" And all at once my seven board members came into my mind.

Yes! Of course! These men were capable and trustworthy, and they had abilities in many areas. God had given them gifts for the furthering of His kingdom, but I needed to give them some scope and authority so they could use those gifts more fully. Why not give each of them a portfolio of responsibility?

Immediately, I jumped up and ran to my office. I wrote their names on a piece of paper and made columns of duties under each name that matched with their areas of giftedness, such as: ushering, inside and outside custodial duties, building maintenance, financial and business records, parking lot, greeters, and so on.

Giving Up Control

At the next board meeting I distributed those lists to the board members, and told them to look them over, and if they felt they wanted to change an item or two I would make the adjustments. I asked them to take the list home and pray about it, and come to the next board meeting with any suggestions.

We worked on those lists for a few months, and when we all agreed on the contents, we publicized them to the congregation. In this way, when anyone had a concern, they would know to first approach the board member whose responsibility it was. If the board member deemed it an appropriate matter for the entire board to consider, it could be placed on their next agenda. Also, I gave the board members authority to ask others in the church to assist them in their area of responsibility, if needed.

Moses' father-in-law gave him similar advice in Exodus 18:13-27, and according to Acts 6, the twelve apostles found they also needed to delegate. I had good Scriptural precedent for delegating the work to the laity!

This system became a marvelous help to me, and released me to *"give (my) attention to prayer and the ministry of the word"* (Acts 6:4, NIV).

This system also helped me organize my board meeting agendas, which had formerly dragged into the midnight hour. When I prepared the board agenda, I would place the initials of the board member responsible after the agenda item. I'd then ask them to do some advance research, and give us a report at the next meeting.

This helped us come to good decisions quickly. I also noticed that, for the most part, the other board members reacted better to ideas that were proposed by a fellow board member than if everything were submitted and pushed by the pastor.

When I learned to delegate in this manner, it was like releasing a big log jam. We used the system for our pastoral staff as well, and it worked wonders for our church. As the administrative functions were taken over by talented laity, and the pastors became more free to pray, seek God, study, and shepherd the flock, our church began to grow once more.

Avoiding Burnout as the Church Grows

When our church grew past 800 or so in attendance, I discovered I needed to take better care of my health. I was beginning to burn out physically, spiritually, and emotionally. I believe the Lord showed me that I not only needed to take annual vacations for rest to refresh my ministry, but that I needed to take a daily vacation.

I divided each day into three parts: forenoon, afternoon, and evening. I decided that if I spent all three of those parts of the day working I was actually sinning. So each day I'd take one of those three parts of the day for leisure and recreation, and do the work of the ministry during the other two. Here is how that worked:

Forenoons were spent in prayer, sermon study, and office. Afternoons were spent at the athletic club and with family, and evenings were spent doing visitation and church meetings.

This is not to say I wouldn't break into my afternoon schedule if emergencies arose, or if there was a funeral or something of that type to attend, but my normal mind-set was to keep the afternoons free of church responsibilities.

I changed something else in my daily schedule about this time. Always, up to this point, Marian had been the one to rise early with our high school children, make them breakfast, and send them off to school with a prayer. This had been her chance to sit down with the children one on one, without interruptions.

But now we had only one child left at home—Boni, our youngest—and her new school was just a mile or so from our house. She could have taken the bus, but the school was on my way to the church. If I got up an hour earlier each morning, we could have breakfast together, and I could drive her to school. I had to work an hour earlier each day, but—well, maybe that helped me feel better about taking the afternoons off!

I began this, thinking it was a way to spend a little more time with a daughter that would soon be gone, but it became a real blessing to me. I loved the ongoing fellowship that we had daily. We didn't have a lot of conversation about anything big—I'm kind of a man of few words—but just having breakfast together and driving that little distance each day was important, I thought. I wanted to be present in her life.

And an added blessing was that we began to have a regular family altar together! This was something that I had always aspired to, but

Giving Up Control

never quite managed to do on a regular basis.

When I was a boy, my parents had set a good example, for every morning without fail we all read the Bible and prayed together before breakfast. But somehow, with our four children, we never could settle on a regular time that worked for everyone. And in spite of all my good intentions, and even preaching some sermons on the subject, our times for family altar were sporadic.

But now, every morning at breakfast with Marian and Boni, we read the Scriptures together and prayed about the coming day. It had taken me a long time, but finally, with my youngest daughter, I'd managed to be faithful in this area.

These changes to my daily schedule helped keep me healthy spiritually, emotionally, and physically; and I think they contributed to my family's health as well.

I believe that is what John is referring to in 3 John 2: *"Beloved, I pray that you may prosper in all things and be in health, just as your soul prospers."*

As the church grows, pastors who wish to succeed discover they must give up some of the control. They learn to seek out and delegate to those they can trust, to those who will do the job well. And they learn to make time to care for themselves and their families.

But it goes without saying that the very best secret of success in God's work is to be a person of prayer.

There are so many things that hinder us in developing a life of prayer. Even growth in the church, though desirable, can choke out a pastor's prayer life if he doesn't learn to share the workload, and if he doesn't make prayer his first priority. Much has been written on the subject, and much is good and helpful, but Jesus gave the clincher in John 15:5 when He said: *"Without Me you can do nothing."*

A pastor who allows his prayer life to atrophy, a pastor who forgets that he can do *nothing* without Christ, is headed for disaster.

Move, and I Will Move

16

Caution Signs

"You were running well; who hindered you from obeying the truth?"

Galatians 5:7 (NASB)

I was driving in the mountains of Norway. The scenery was incredibly beautiful. But the road was narrow, with many hairpin turns, and steep precipices just a few inches from the edge of the road. I can tell you that I paid closer attention to my driving than to the view!

I was unfamiliar with the road. I had no way of knowing what dangers might be just ahead. But the Norwegian road crews knew, and they had set up guard rails, and caution signs, and speed limits. If obeyed, these signs were assurance to me that I could make this unfamiliar journey safely.

Likewise, on our road of life there are many danger points which are called temptations to sin. God's word identifies the trouble spots with markers, or caution signs—scriptures that warn us to watch out, to slow down. And the more familiar we are with the word of God, the more we read it and memorize it and hide it in our hearts, the more it will be there in our minds when we need it most.

God has placed hundreds of warnings in His word to keep His servants from yielding to Satan's temptations. When I was very young, attending Vacation Bible School, I memorized Psalms 119:11: *"Your word have I hid in my heart that I might not sin against You."*

As I was growing up I adopted a plan to put to memory some key verses of scripture. I found from experience that when I was tempted to sin, the Holy Spirit brought one of those cautionary verses to my mind. Just like a red flag or a warning sign, the verse caused me to slow down and think about what might be just ahead, and take the proper precautions to avoid the hazard.

Whenever I look back into my past, I recall how thankful I am that the Holy Spirit brought the inspired word of God to my remembrance! Had I ignored God's warning signs, I would have completely ruined my life of ministry.

Satan will prompt us to sin—that is something you can count on. But the Spirit inspired word of God will raise a standard against the temptation. That was the secret of Jesus' victory when Satan brought Him to the wilderness of temptation. He simply answered Satan each time, "It is written."

This is the sword of the Spirit—the one offensive weapon in our armor, as described in Ephesians 6:10-17. I urge every Christian to devise a plan to memorize scripture in a consistent manner—and most especially pastors.

Have you ever been at the scene of a terrible car accident? I have. I remember one such scene in particular, where a father, mother, and child were killed. We witnesses stood silent, looking on helplessly at the wreckage. The squad cars arrived with flashing lights, and the ambulance medics were ready to give aid, but it was too late. The car had smashed through the guardrail and gone off the embankment, and there was nothing left of the family but broken, lifeless bodies.

Only sad tasks remained—cleaning up the roadside, carrying the bodies to the morgue, and worst of all, notifying the family and friends of the death of their loved ones.

But even more sad, to me, is the terrible destruction that occurs when a pastor goes off the road, spiritually. I have had the painful task, on occasion, of witnessing such wrecks, and helping to clean up the mess.

But these spiritual wrecks do not usually happen all at once, though

Caution Signs

it may seem that way to outsiders. No—in the innermost heart of the pastor, there are usually many warning signs that trouble is coming. When these are ignored, although the ministry may still look wonderful on the surface, it will not last long.

"The fear of the Lord is the beginning of knowledge..."
(Proverbs 1:7a)

The Bible is not just a book of warnings. It is full of "go" signs—"This Way", or "Enter Here", that point us in the right direction.

"Joe"[8] had a good beginning. His parents followed the biblical direction sign in Proverbs 1:7 and brought him and his siblings up in the fear, or reverence, of the Lord. As Joe grew to manhood, he felt the call of the Lord to become a minister of the gospel. He enrolled at an Assemblies of God University and became an honor student.

For a few years after graduation Joe worked with seasoned AG pastors doing youth ministries, until a small AG church asked him to become their pastor. He began his ministry in that little church praying that his small congregation might be built up in the Spirit of the Lord. He sought the Lord with sincerity. He felt honored to have a congregation to shepherd. He humbly prayed for the power of the Holy Spirit to renew his strength, so that he could somehow carry the message of salvation.

Joe's wife, "Mary", loved him and delighted in him and promoted him wherever she could. Joe loved Mary and once said: "I love you so much Mary, sometimes it hurts."

Joe was diligent to contact every member of his little church. He made a list of when he would do it. He also made another list of prospects in order to build attendance. He attended every meeting of the City Council to find out what was happening in the community. He also met with the merchants and got acquainted with them.

One day his wife Mary called him at 5:00 p.m. to say that dinner was ready. Then Joe remembered he hadn't eaten all day, he'd been so excited about building his church. As the little church grew, there were

---

[8]Names used in this chapter are not the real names.

more calls for help which took Joe away from his family from early morning until late at night.

> **"But if anyone does not provide for his own,**
> **and especially for those of his household,**
> **he has denied the faith and is worse**
> **than an unbeliever."**
>
> *(1 Timothy 5:8)*

This caution sign is often misunderstood. The word "provide" means more than providing room and board. A good provider also gives attention to the emotional needs of his family. He nurtures his loved ones – and puts them in his schedule happily.

Joe's wife Mary was neglected because Joe was always too busy to spend time with her. At Christmas she became lonesome for her parents as she remembered the happy times growing up, but her husband didn't seem to notice or care. As time passed, Joe gave more and more attention to the church work which pressed on him, and less and less to his family. The little church was filling up, but Mary felt a check in her spirit and didn't know why.

To make matters worse, Joe began to neglect his young son as well. "Jim" often begged his father to come out and play soccer with him, but Joe invariably refused; he always had another meeting to attend. As Jim grew older, he began to see the church as something that took his father away from him. He felt engaged in a battle for his father's attention that he could never win. As Jim understood, painfully, that he would never be a priority for his father, he gradually lost interest in the church and the things of the Lord.

Mary could see that they were heading for serious trouble. But Joe became annoyed whenever his wife tried to talk to him about her concerns. After all, he was doing the Lord's work, wasn't he? Joe decided that Mary just wasn't as spiritual and on fire for God as he was—and was probably overreacting as well.

> **"...But fools despise wisdom and instruction."**
>
> *(Proverbs 1:7b)*

Watch out! A spouse's complaints are a guardrail—don't ignore

Caution Signs

them. She can see things that you may be blinded to. That is why God gave her to you—to help you. Too many men cut off their own right hand by refusing to listen to the concerns and wise counsel of their spouse.

A child's unhappiness is a danger sign—falling rock ahead, avalanche area, sudden flash floods. It may come to nothing. Or it may be catastrophic. But ignore this warning sign at your peril.

Joe's relationship with his wife and son continued to deteriorate. The family experienced crisis after crisis in a long series of unresolved differences.

Meanwhile, Joe had great compassion and seemingly endless energy for the families of his church. He created activities to attract more young couples and their children, and added fun by serving popcorn, sodas, and showing movies. His ministry at the little church flourished so that the congregation grew, which got the attention of the board from a rather large church looking for a pastor.

When driving along a residential street or ambling country lane, the pace is slow, and the driver has lots of time to react. Accidents tend to be more minor, and damage to the car or the people within is more easily fixed.

But as soon as you move onto the freeway, the potential for dangerous situations is greater. The driver must be even more alert and responsible at higher speeds. Until you can drive safely and well at lower speeds, you shouldn't attempt to take on the challenge of high speed driving, exciting though it may be.

Joe thought he was doing well at his "residential driving"—pastoring a small church. But he was neglecting to maintain and care for his personal life, for his wife and son. There was a wobble in his steering, and it took greater and greater effort to keep his car on the road.

Still, he was contacted by the search committee of this large congregation and was elected to become their shepherd. This was freeway driving! He ignored the pesky steering problem, and determined to take this rapid promotion. After all, he had accomplished a lot already, and he had plans to do much more. His

Move, and I Will Move

predecessors had pioneered and built the church to become strong and solid. It had a strong testimony in a modest sized city and was well known in the surrounding community.

> **"Therefore let him who thinks he stands take heed lest he fall."**
>
> *(1 Corinthians 10:12)*

As Joe hit his stride as pastor of the prestigious new church, he became aware that he was more than meeting expectations. But this verse warns us to be even more watchful when things are going well.

When a minister is successful by the world's standards (high attendance, good offerings, church growth, respect in the community and among his peers), he is tempted to attribute his success to his own personal gifts. Little by little, he ceases to fear and reverence God. He no longer trembles in the presence of God; he no longer feels himself to be inadequate, desperately relying on the Holy Spirit to get him through.

> **"For I say...to everyone who is among you, not to think of himself more highly than he ought to think."**
>
> *(Romans 12:3)*

This caution sign is easy to ignore when we are naturally gifted. Joe began living and working and depending upon his own personal abilities, for they seemed fully adequate for the task. Thinking that his charismatic personality and ability to please were all he needed, he neglected his relationship with God.

For awhile, Joe was able to continue the appearance of a strong ministry. He was a good communicator, and his messages were scriptural and spoke to the needs of his people. He especially enjoyed their praise, which gave him a sense of security in his career.

> **"But you are a chosen generation, a royal priesthood, a holy nation, His own special people, that you may proclaim the praises of Him who called you out of darkness into His marvelous light."**
>
> *(1 Peter 2:9)*

These words of the Apostle Peter slap us back into wakefulness.

Caution Signs

Take heed, he says—this is the reason you were called! Not so that others can praise you and say how wonderful you are, but to proclaim the praises of God.

Still, it is possible to give audible praise to God and yet have a rising spirit of power and admiration of our own abilities. Unknowingly, Joe's heart began to fill with pride and self-satisfaction.

> **"A man's pride will bring him low,
> but the humble in spirit will retain honor."**
>
> *(Proverbs 29:23)*

Joe's growing pride, and neglect of his relationship with God, brought him only inner emptiness. But Joe did a lot of counseling with women in the congregation. He gave them his full attention, and showed a warmth and kindness that impressed them. The women responded with heartfelt words: "Oh, pastor, you help me so much!" and "I so appreciate your warmth and love."

Joe's warmth and love did not extend to his own wife and son, however. And he wasn't wise enough to give the praise to God for helping him in his counseling work. Instead, he used the acclaim of these women as a way of filling his own needs.

> **"But they do all their deeds to be noticed by men...
> and they love the place of honor at banquets..."**
>
> *(Matthew 23:5a, 6a, NASB)*

Those who knew Joe well began to see evidence that he wasn't seeking God's approval. He showed a growing appetite for compliments from his people. He seemed to almost bask in their appreciation.

This was completely predictable. Since he was no longer sustained by a deep relationship with God, Joe quite naturally turned to other things. He sought to fill the barrenness in his soul by pleasing people and winning their praise.

But, of course, this wasn't enough. Joe, of all people, should have known that no substitute for God will satisfy for long. Still, he did not humble himself and seek God when he felt empty inside. Instead, he turned to pornography.

Move, and I Will Move

> **"When pride comes, then comes shame;
> but with the humble is wisdom."**
>
> *(Proverbs 11:2)*

If only Joe had heeded this warning in Proverbs! But his pride could not admit his mistake.

In proportion as he had come to think highly of himself and his abilities, he was less and less inclined to accept instruction. Caution signs that might have made him pause a few years ago no longer had the same effect. They might be good for others, he thinks, but he is special—unusually gifted—and an exception to the general rule. Things that would hurt others, won't have any effect on him.

And so Joe continued to seek out pornography on the internet. Although he knew it was wrong, his conscience had become callused over time, for he had continually ignored God's warning signs in scripture.

> **"Obey those who rule over you,
> and be submissive, for they watch out for your souls,
> as those who must give account."**
>
> *(Hebrews 13:17a)*

Whether a secret addiction or a lusting thought, being accountable and opening our lives to others is a healthy spiritual exercise, and lives and ministry can be rescued before it is too late.

The secret sin of viewing pornography behind closed doors has become a vicious addiction for many, damaging relationships and separating Christians from their heavenly Father. The clandestine use of Internet pornography strongly calls for every minister of the gospel to belong to an accountability group; it provides human feedback which filters don't.

Joe knew what he should do—confess his sin and get help from those who were in spiritual authority over him. But he did not want to do it.

> **"The way of a fool is right in his own eyes,
> but he who heeds counsel is wise."**
>
> *(Proverbs 12:15)*

Joe didn't bother to take this caution sign very seriously. It would be too humiliating, he thought, to confess his addiction to

Caution Signs

pornography. He had no interest in joining a group of men that held each other accountable for their lifestyle. Any problems he had, he could handle on his own, without submitting himself to anyone.

After all, he was the senior pastor of a prestigious church. He was a successful man, sought after for speaking engagements and pointed out at conferences. He, of all people, was self-sufficient—he hardly needed to spend time running around asking for help from God or anyone else.

So Joe hung on to his pride—and chose the path of a fool. The result turned out to be catastrophic for him, his family, his church, his friends, and the kingdom of God.

> **"Even so you too outwardly appear righteous to men, but inwardly you are full of hypocrisy and lawlessness."**
> *(Matthew 23:28)*

Stop! Verses that accuse and condemn are stop signs in no uncertain terms. But those who ignore many cautions along the way, will have trouble taking stop signs seriously.

The secret meetings went on for months, and no one was the wiser. Joe's desperate attempt to fill the emptiness inside had finally led to the devastating sin of adultery.

He had become very sly, very adept at hiding what was really going on in his life. Joe had been an able and gifted man—but now his God-given abilities were all used to create a facade behind which he could hide. Wife, family, congregation—all were fooled. But at last something slipped. Rumors crept out, and people began to suspect he was being unfaithful to his wife.

Finally, Joe was confronted with the rumors—but he denied them vehemently.

> **"And all liars shall have their part in the lake which burns with fire and brimstone, which is the second death."**
> *(Revelation 21:8b)*

Joe was long past the point where he was paying attention to caution signs or even stop signs in God's word. He had gone too far down the wrong road, and yet he continued on the same path.

Evidence was brought to his overseers. When Joe was confronted again, he unequivocally denied the allegations. Even his wife, who had suffered from his neglect for years, made statements supporting his innocence. Finally, Joe was given a letter.

His own handwriting was on the page. It had been written to his lady friend. And the contents proved his guilt, all too clearly.

> **"...you have sinned against the Lord; and be sure your sin will find you out."**
>
> *(Numbers 32:23b)*

"Well, gentlemen," said Joe, now that he had been found out, "what do you want me to do?"

The leader of the district looked him in the eye. "I want your credentials. Furthermore, you won't be able to return to the pulpit of your church. Your ministry is over."

> **"Pride goes before destruction."**
>
> *(Proverbs 16:18a)*

One of the saddest things in the world is to see a once promising ministry shattered because of moral failure. And pastors cannot plead ignorance as to the many caution signs in scripture. After all, it's their job to tell others about the warnings!

But there have been some pastors in our fellowship who, while calling out warnings to others, have taken their own eyes off the road. As a result, they made mistakes that sent them spinning off the edge, and destroyed their effectiveness as ministers of the gospel. And a sign is put up on the roadway—a cross, a wreath, or some other symbol to let us know that a tragedy occurred here, in the hopes that this unmistakable warning will witness to others going down the same road.

Like a steep mountainside on which the snow piles up, snowfall after snowfall, an erring pastor can cover up his sin with a blanket of busy church work and good deeds. It may look wonderful on the surface, but the whole slope is unstable in the extreme—and the slightest disturbance to the crust sends the whole mess sliding down, causing massive destruction.

Caution Signs

But it doesn't have to happen that way, for we have been given the word of God. Every time Jesus used the "sword of the Spirit," God's word, He emerged victorious over Satan. If we follow Jesus' example, we will also live successfully.

If Joe had only paid attention to the numerous caution signs, all leading to stop signs! If only he had thought about what his sinful actions would do to his life and ministry, to his wife, his children, his parents and grandparents, to all of his relatives, to the people of his church and community, and the far reaching cause of Christ.

If only. Don't let this be your epitaph.

Move, and I Will Move

17

Move, and I Will Move

"Now faith is the substance of things hoped for, the evidence of things not seen."

Hebrews 11:1

We were on our knees when God spoke.

The board members and I had all been praying together in the basement of the old Kimball schoolhouse, trying to discern God's will in the matter of relocating. In seven years our congregation had grown from the original 27 to about 125 typically attending on a Sunday, and we were bursting at the seams.

A property had been found at 94th and Portland that looked good—but the cost was $20,200. We needed to raise the whole amount, not just a down payment, and there was no money in the treasury.

The cement floor was hard on our knees, but it didn't matter. We were earnestly seeking God, and the murmur of our voices rose and fell as we prayed, each man in his own way. And then suddenly one voice was raised above all the rest, loud and commanding.

"Move, and I will move!"

It was electrifying. We opened our eyes and stared at Lyle May, from whose mouth the words had come. But he didn't say anything more.

We didn't really even discuss what had happened, as I recall. It was

The old Kimball Schoolhouse bursts at the seams. (Marian and Arvid Kingsriter at far right.)

clear to everyone in the room that God had spoken through Lyle's prophetic words, and we all understood the meaning.

God wanted us to take a step of faith in this matter. If we did that, then He would act; it was as simple as that.

We all got up and sat on our chairs. Someone made a motion that we buy the property, someone else seconded it, and we voted unanimously to put the need before the congregation. By the next Sunday, someone had drawn a big thermometer, maybe twelve feet tall, with dollar amounts instead of degrees. We put it up on the right hand side of the platform so people could watch the red go up as the money was raised.

I remember John Bonstrom saying, "Arvid, we can do this, we can *do* this!" He was a very positive man, full of faith, and a generous giver—and he was right. It only took a couple of weeks before the whole amount was pledged.

The Divine Principle at Work

Hebrews 11:1 tells us: *"Now faith is the substance of things hoped for, the evidence of things not seen."* That gives us a big difference between the believer and the unbeliever, right there.

The unbeliever says, "I'll have to see it before I'll believe it." But the believer says, "I'll have to believe it *before* I see it." He decides to take God at His word by acting upon it.

Victory does not happen to us while we passively wait. Still, people who take the initiative by taking steps of faith toward a certain objective are often labeled as 'risk takers', especially if they don't have a clear prescribed set of step-by-step instructions .

Move, and I Will Move

And yet, when does God ever give a whole series of instructions, neatly laid out? It doesn't seem to be the way He usually works. God likes us to show, by our actions, that we trust Him—and then He promises to give us all that we need.

Joshua chapter three illustrates this divine principle. The children of Israel were headed for the promised land, but they had to cross the river Jordan, and it was in full flood—overflowing its banks, verse 15 says. And God's instructions were simple; the priests should lead the way, carrying the ark of the covenant, and they should step right into the river. When they took that step of faith, God promised to act.

And He did. Just as soon as their feet touched the water, it rolled back from either side, and there was dry ground for the crossing.

In the basement of the old Kimball schoolhouse, God had given us our instructions, too. That prophecy, "Move, and I will move," became marching orders for Bloomington Assembly from then on.

Within a year, we held groundbreaking ceremonies for the new building. Eight years later we were holding two Sunday morning services and bursting at the seams again, so we added a new sanctuary seating 500. And four years after that, we were again holding two services, and getting crowded once more.

It was time to reproduce!

We add a new sanctuary at 94th and Portland. The mural is of the sower and the seed.

Move, and I Will Move

After Growth and Maturity Comes Reproduction

I had read an article in the early 1970's that influenced me strongly. The author said emphatically that no church should have over 500 members. Up to that number, he felt that you could have adequate ministries for all your people; but beyond that, you couldn't meet everyone's needs.

His answer to the problem of a growing church was simple—reproduce! Use your church's resources to plant a new congregation in the community, he said—and the part of me that was a farmer, and loved to plant new seed, really responded to this.

But this wasn't the way things were done in the Minnesota Assemblies of God District at the time. The decision to plant a new church would typically come from the district leadership, and they would decide where the church would go, and how everything would be handled.

But I have to admit that this process was a slow one at the time. I could imagine it taking years, if we went through the usual procedure; and in the meantime, visitors were driving in our parking lot on Sunday mornings, and driving right out again, because they couldn't find enough parking.

Our problem was acute, and I not only wanted to plant a new church—I wanted to siphon off some people! It was exciting to think that people from our congregation could start a work in their own community, and become leaders in a brand new congregation.

But if I went ahead and did this on my own, I knew I would be considered a maverick. There wasn't any rule against it, as far as I knew, but it definitely wasn't the approved method.

So, although we had a few families coming from the suburb of Eden Prairie, and I had begun to feel that perhaps we should plant a "daughter" church there, I hesitated.

It took an altar call to convince me to act.

In 1973 I was attending our General Council in Miami Beach, Florida, when General Superintendent Thomas F. Zimmerman spoke about the need to plant more churches. He made a special plea for pastors to take a step of faith, and commit to leading their congregations to reproduce—to 'mother' a new daughter church.

Move, and I Will Move

Eden Prairie, and the issue of planting a church there, was already so much on my heart; and now here was no less a person than the General Superintendent of the Assemblies of God urging me on! Surely, even though there were those in the Minnesota district who would disapprove, I had been given the go-ahead. The Holy Spirit flooded my heart with a longing to respond, and I got up and walked down the aisle.

When I got home, I told the board about my commitment.

They said fine, let's do it—but we didn't do anything right away, and months went by.

Finally it dawned on me that, although I didn't exactly know what to do or how to begin, I had to start a move in that direction. It was back to the "Move, and I will move" prophecy, and as far as I was concerned, it still held true.

We had a couple from Eden Prairie that was attending at Bloomington Assembly, Jim and Sandi Robertson, and they always sat in the back row. I looked at them one Sunday, and knew I had to talk to Jim.

He was a police officer, and he was one of those guys who knew everyone. He knew who to contact, what was going on, and how to get things done. So I told him of my dream to plant a church in his suburb, and asked him to take me on a sightseeing tour of Eden Prairie.

He drove me all around. He introduced me to the mayor, and to other people who were responsible for making decisions for the city, and in the end we found some property for sale. It had a church building already on it, from another denomination's failed attempt to start a new church, and the price was $150,000.

We scheduled a special business meeting of the Bloomington Assembly members and voted on resolutions: to become a 'mother church', to float a bond issue to pay for the property, and to call a pastor who would come to Bloomington Assembly and solicit people to be part of the new Eden Prairie congregation. Then we invited all those interested to a dinner where they could voice their questions and concerns.

About this time, I was driving down the road toward Eden Prairie, when suddenly fear flooded my mind. What if this grand plan didn't work out? We were going out on a limb, I knew, and there were doubtless some who disapproved already. What would people in the district think of me if we failed?

It is interesting that the fear was all about me. I wasn't thinking about the damage to the kingdom of God if we failed—I was thinking about the damage to Arvid Kingsriter's reputation!

I decided that this fear was not from God, but from the Enemy, and as such I should resist it. So I did. I determined to stop worrying about myself and what people would think, and instead press on to accomplish the task God had set before me.

A few weeks later we asked Rev. Wesley and Diane Brooks to become the new pastors. We had them preach at Bloomington Assembly at both services on a Sunday. At the evening altar time, all those interested in identifying with the new daughter church were invited to come forward for commitment and dedication.

The vacated building we had purchased had been completely stripped of all its furniture including chairs, tables, desks, piano, and so on. We made a survey of what was needed to conduct Sunday School and Church Services, and the cost totaled $10,000.

I thought about Inez Olson in Little Falls, a lady that had always had a heart for the Lord's work, and told her of our need. Bless her generous heart, she gave the $10,000, and the furnishings were quickly purchased and delivered.

The opening services were announced, Bloomington Assembly loaned Sunday School teachers for a period of six months, and the church was on its way!

I didn't know exactly what I was doing or how to go about planting a new church, but we all learned as we went. The thing we really didn't have a pattern for was how to support the baby church at first, and yet gradually release the control as the church matured.

A text that I found useful was Psalms 32:8: *"I will instruct you (says the Lord) and guide you along the best pathway for your life; I will advise you and watch your progress"* (LB).

Instruct, guide, advise and watch the progress. This is not only how the Lord deals with us; this is also a blueprint for raising our own children. And this text helped me understand the biblical way to lead the Eden Prairie church into maturity.

Instruction

The first step is instruction. This is something you do preemptively, before problems arise. The wise parent thinks of things the child will someday need to know, and teaches them.

Here's an example. Through my life, I had turned to the Bible again and again, finding direction, comfort, and refreshment for my spirit. I wanted my children to have the same benefit, so I began teaching them to memorize scripture at a young age.

We used little flashcards, and they got a dime at the end of the week if they could repeat the verse and reference correctly. Review verses from the previous month, said correctly, got them a nickel each, and they could even get a penny for each review verse from the previous year.

It was a kind of game, with rewards they could understand; but of course the greatest reward was that they were hiding the treasure of God's word in their hearts. Fifty-two verses a year adds up! I knew that in the future, these verses would be a rich resource for them.

I don't think the staff at Bloomington Assembly had any such riches of instruction to offer the fledgling Eden Prairie Assembly, but we did have a little experience, and a willingness to share what we knew; and of course we were supporting them financially as well.

So for the first year, we had pastor Wesley Brooks attend our staff meetings every week; he gave us a report on how things were going, and our experienced staff was a resource for him. We knew the area, the people in his new congregation, and the problems that were likely to arise, and we passed this information on to him.

Guidance

Step two, guidance, is given when uncertainty comes into the picture, and helps to clarify the proper direction. Psalms 32:8 goes on to say *"(I will) guide you along the best pathway for your life"* (LB).

There are many pathways our children can follow, but they do not always have the judgment to discern the best way to go.

Parents can lend their experience and wisdom. As children are making life's decisions, the parents and other counselors are there to guide them; and gradually, over time, the child takes on more and more of the responsibility.

After a few months at Eden Prairie, pastor Wesley Brooks was getting to know his congregation. So with his help, we appointed an advisory board of three people from his congregation. These people were invited, along with Wes, to come to our regular board meetings.

This was our way of beginning to shift responsibility away from us and over to them; to take their input into account, and to offer guidance as issues came up and decisions needed to be made.

Advice

Advice, the third step in the scriptural method outlined in Psalms 32, is by definition optional—the recipient of the advice doesn't have to take it. Advice comes into play more often as our children approach adulthood, and once the child has reached maturity, the wise parent only gives it when specifically requested!

But if there has been a good relationship in the past, the son or daughter may well ask for advice now and then. They are wise enough to value experience, and secure enough to know that asking for advice doesn't mean they have to take it.

Pastor Wes Brooks received a call to pastor another church before Eden Prairie Assembly became fully independent. When a new pastor was invited to consider an offer from Eden Prairie, he came and asked me what was obviously an important question to him. How long, he wondered, was Bloomington Assembly planning to call the shots for Eden Prairie?

"Bob," I said, "we're ready to shift all that to you, just as soon as you're ready to take it on."

He was happy to hear that, and he had been hoping to hear that. He needed to know that he would be able to take charge as senior pastor, as soon as his congregation was ready to assume financial responsibility. And as I recall, it was about six months later that they had their organizational meting, elected officers, and voted to assume full responsibility for the pastor's salary.

The pastor now and then still consulted with me, and asked for advice, but the daughter church had grown up and left the nest—and that's how it is supposed to be.

Watching Their Progress

This fourth step is a delight. What a joy to see a child grow up and become independent! Special events mark the path to maturity; a graduation from high school or college, a wedding, and the dedication of a new baby are all joyous occasions, and a good time to reflect upon the past teaching, guidance and advice that all helped this once dependent person grow into a fully functioning adult.

And one of the most rewarding things is to see your children passing on, to their own children, the instruction you have given them.

My daughter Boni is now a high school teacher. But when she was in high school herself, we studied a devotional book together. We also, together with Marian, had a family altar time in the mornings. I had never managed to do this regularly before, but somehow with Boni all my good intentions came together in action. The wonderful blessing was not only that we spent this time of spiritual instruction together, but the resulting fruit in her life. She, now that she has a family of her own, has made it a priority to have regular devotional and prayer times with them, and it's a joy for me to see that.

At Bloomington Assembly, we watched with joy and thanksgiving as Eden Prairie Assembly held the special events that marked its progress. Although the church building was already built, and so we did not have a groundbreaking ceremony or the laying of a cornerstone, there was a church dedication, and installation of their pastors.

In 1976, just two years after we had brought this church into the world, Eden Prairie was on its own. Still, we loved to watch their progress, and in future years we were invited to many more special events.

We Have Another Daughter

Some months after Eden Prairie Assembly was officially on its own, a man walked into church one Sunday morning and stopped me in the entrance. "Say, Pastor, you know I'm from Prior Lake. Can we do in Prior Lake what we did in Eden Prairie?"

I felt a little like a young mother feels about having another baby too soon after the first. "We can do it," I said slowly, "but you'll have to wait awhile." I just wasn't ready to plunge into that again—but he had planted a seed in my mind.

And in a matter of months, as the sanctuary got more and more crowded, I approached this man.

"Let's have a meeting out at your house," I said. "We can invite everyone that comes to this church from Prior Lake, and see if they'd be interested in starting a new church out there."

So that's what we did. We must have had fifteen or twenty people at that first meeting. We talked about starting a church in Prior Lake, and they said they were very interested. We had a time of prayer, and then I passed around some pieces of paper.

"Don't write your name on it," I said. "But if you're sincere about wanting an Assemblies of God church planted in Prior Lake, then show me how interested you really are. Write down the amount of money you'd give as a weekly tithe if we started this church."

I watched them writing. It was another case of "Move, and I will move," I thought. These people weren't just writing down numbers. They were stepping out in faith, just like the priests stepping into the Jordan and trusting God to give them a place to walk.

I totaled the numbers, and it came to $350 a week. That was enough, at that date, to pay a pastor and rent some space to start.

And now I felt like the young mother who still thought the new baby had come too soon—but when it arrived, she couldn't be happier. I think I had a big grin on my face as I said, "It looks like we're ready to go!"

We searched for and found a pastor who felt led to shepherd this core group of believers, and they held their first services in a school. Later, the Bloomington Assembly board loaned them $30,000 (from the Arthur Erickson memorial fund, a fund that had been created for the purpose of planting new churches) to purchase property on which a church building was constructed. The Prior Lake Assembly has grown, and is today a strong, vibrant congregation.

Planting a church through a local congregation, rather than under district leadership, made for a very personal connection. It created a mentoring relationship with the daughter church that seemed to work out very well.

We probably didn't do everything right, but what we did do was successful enough that other churches followed our example afterwards—not only in Minnesota, but all over the nation. We were even written up in the *Pentecostal Evangel,* and there was a picture of our board members on the front cover, praying over a map of the communities surrounding Bloomington.

Cover of the Pentecostal Evangel, January 1977. The church board prays over the site of the next satellite church we will sponsor.

I Examine My Assumptions

Church planting is exciting, and two daughter churches in three years was moving fast, even for me! I suppose I thought that Bloomington Assembly would just keep starting more churches in the future. After all, I was still operating under the theory I had read about in the article on church growth; namely, that a church should never get above 500 members.

But in the late 70's I attended a minister's conference in Chicago. The speaker was an Assemblies of God pastor named Dr. Paul Yonggi Cho, and he not only challenged that theory of mine—he demolished it.

Move, and I Will Move

18

I Will Get You Ready

"A man's heart plans his way, but the Lord directs his steps."
Proverbs 16:9

I had a bad cold, and I was sitting by myself at the minister's conference. I didn't want to give my cold to anyone—or at least that was the reason I gave.

The real reason was that I wanted to be quiet, to be alone with my thoughts, and allow the Lord speak to speak to me in His own way.

I suspected that God was going to do some rearranging of my theories at this conference. I had known that ever since I heard of Dr. Cho and his 200,000 member church. But the whole idea of a congregation that large was overwhelming to me. How did this man do it? How had God prepared him to pastor so many people?

Dr. Cho's Story

Dr. Paul Yonggi Cho had graduated from a Korean Assemblies of God Bible School in 1958. He began his first church during the chaos following the Korean conflict, when people were homeless and sick all over the city of Seoul. Families were separated because of the military zones, and often had no idea where their loved ones were. Many were living in cardboard boxes, and the lucky ones had a little plastic sheeting to keep off the rain.

It was in this setting that God had spoken to Dr. Cho very clearly, saying: "I can do everything my people will ever need. I see what their needs are. They need to learn how to pray until they break through and touch me, and that's what I want you to do."

Dr. Cho took this message back to the Yoido Full Gospel Church—a little group of believers that met in a tent. He said, "We are going to come every day, and we are going to pray under the tent until we break through and touch God."

The people said, "If we are hungry, and don't have any food, we won't have time to pray. We will have to go and find food, but this is what we pay you for—so you pray for us."

But Dr. Cho said "No, this message was for all of us. Come to the tent when you come, leave when you have to, but we are going to pray together." And so they did.

Dr. Cho's mother-in-law was at the tent during the day, and prayed with everyone who came. And at night, Dr. Cho knelt in front of the altar and prayed. They did this every day for three and a half years, in all kinds of weather; and then suddenly, on an ordinary day without any warning, God broke through.

Wonderful things happened; there were so many healings that they became commonplace. People were healed just sitting in the service, without anyone praying for them. There was a man who was stone deaf, and suddenly in the midst of an evening service he began to shout, "I can hear! I can hear!"

People around him looked at him and smiled, as if to acknowledge that yes, a wonderful thing had happened, but then they went right back to listening to Dr. Cho, because a healing like that was a normal occurrence.

Of course, with things like this happening, the church began to grow. And as it grew, with the Holy Spirit's guidance, Dr. Cho developed ways to minister to people in small groups within the large congregation.

He shared all those ways with us during that conference. He said it was nothing that couldn't be found in the book of Acts, but he gave a lot of illustrations to show us what had worked for him and how it worked. And as I sat there, with my stuffy head and my cough, I began to clearly see that I had been limiting God.

After all, it wasn't God who had said a church shouldn't grow beyond 500. It was just the writer of an article that had impressed me.

I didn't regret having started two daughter churches. For all I knew, we might start some more in the future. But for now, I just felt as if God had taken the lid off the box.

Looking for Direction

I had attended the conference with my son-in-law, Jerry Strandquist, who at that time was the senior pastor of Farmington Assembly of God. As we drove back to Minnesota together, I remember how anxious I was to get home so I could get started and implement all I had learned. The miles just crawled by!

Once at home, I met with the board and shared the change in my thinking. They seemed to say, in effect, "Go ahead, let's go, sic 'em!" So we appointed a relocation committee. If we were going to allow the church to grow, we couldn't do it in our present cramped location.

That relocation committee had representatives in it from every gender and age group among the membership, including some in high school. We met several times for brainstorming sessions, and had a free-for-all, talking about ideas for growth and how to expand. Everyone seemed excited about the idea of growth.

Some of the proposals I thought were a little ridiculous... someone wanted a swimming pool, as I recall. We had to scale back on some of those ideas, but on the whole, it was good to have everyone's input.

Then came a long process of looking for a suitable property. This was in the early 80s, and Bloomington didn't have many properties with the amount of vacant land we needed. Our relocation committee led us into purchasing several different properties, none of which were perfect, but which they had felt we should snap up before someone else got them. I was at a loss as to which one we should pursue.

Then Glen Gilbertson, a long time member of Bloomington Assembly, gave me a call. "I've got a property I think you should look at," he told me. "It's the vacant Cedarcrest Elementary School, and I think it's got everything we need."

My head started to ache at that. We already owned three properties, and our money was tied up while we decided which one to use. The last thing I wanted was to throw yet another one into the mix!

But Glen was pretty insistent, and so I went along and saw the property. Interestingly enough, the school was just a few blocks away from 86th and Cedar, where Bloomington Assembly had gotten its start. In fact, Cedarcrest had been built to replace the old Kimball schoolhouse that we had used as our church.

The property looked good, but I was still confused. I hadn't felt right in my spirit about acquiring all the properties we now owned, but had let myself be guided by the committee. And now we had to make a decision, and I hardly thought acquiring a fourth property was going to help matters.

I Will Get You Ready

As always when faced with a difficult decision, I headed for the woods. I walked and prayed, and at last came to a fallen tree and sat down.

My heart was very heavy. I was crying as I prayed, begging God to give me some specific directions for the future of our church. And suddenly, in a flash, I saw a vision of a new sanctuary that was attached to the south side of the Cedarcrest Elementary School.

That vision was brief, but it was very clear. I knew in my spirit that God was directing our church to move to that property.

When there is clarity of vision, the energy follows! I told our church board, and they authorized a special meeting of the congregation to sell the other properties we had acquired, and to purchase the Cedarcrest property. We voted unanimously to make the move.

In August of 1982 we began to hold services in the cafeteria of the school. In March of 1983 we approved the plan for the new sanctuary. The following month we had a groundbreaking ceremony, and construction began.

There were workmen all over the place during the summer, and I mostly tried to stay out of their way. But one day, after everyone had

I Will Get You Ready

gone, I walked into the sanctuary to look around.

The walls and roof were up, and the balcony was built, but the floor was still earth. I stood where the pulpit would be and looked at the huge spaces where people would be sitting—there was room for 2,000—and I became frightened. I said aloud, "Arvid, you're not ready for this!"

Suddenly there was a still small voice within me, saying, "Take a sabbatical, and I will get you ready."

I hardly knew what a sabbatical was, but I knew God had once again given me direction. I called a meeting of our church board and told them of my experience.

One of them said, "How long do you want the sabbatical to last?"

"I don't have any idea," I admitted.

"Well, 40 days is often a scriptural period of time," he suggested.

That sounded good to me. And after some discussion, the board voted unanimously to continue my salary and pay all the expenses for travel and so on that I would incur.

The sanctuary was going to be completed in early 1984, so I took the last 40 days of 1983 for my sabbatical. I really had no idea what to do with the time, except to ask the Lord for further direction. So I spent the first week at our cabin, alone. I fasted, prayed, and wrote down everything that the Lord was telling me.

Bloomington Assembly of God, now called Cedar Valley Church. This is the finished sanctuary at the new location on 86th and Bloomington Avenue.

Next, I visited a number of large churches in the southern states, talking to the pastors, deacons, business administrators, secretaries and custodians. I took voluminous notes. Then I spent the final days of my sabbatical back at our cabin, arranging the ideas that I felt would work for us.

I met with the staff and board, and shared my findings. And on February 19, when I stood at the pulpit in the new sanctuary and looked out at all the people, I knew God had kept His promise. I felt ready.

Ready or Not, Here it Comes

I was ready to pastor a large church, but I was also 63 years old. I knew that retirement was in my future.

I also knew that it was important for me to stick around for awhile. We'd just built a new sanctuary, and taken on a great deal of debt. According to all I had heard or read about the subject, a pastor who implements a building program should stay put for a good five to six years afterwards.

People need a sense of continuity and confidence during a time of change. Until I had a sense that the church was solidly on its feet after this big upheaval, and the new people who were coming to the church were well integrated into the congregation, I didn't want to leave.

But I was slowing down, and I could feel it. I was thinking ahead with a certain amount of longing for the time when I could lay down the burden of leadership.

In spite of my weariness, though, the challenges I was facing didn't decrease. If anything, the load seemed to be increasing, and I found myself doing battle on several fronts.

It was a good thing I had learned to pray. Because if I had not been able to fall on my knees before God and draw strength from that inexhaustible well, I would have been lost.

Battle in the Public Arena

Of course there always had been challenges. One of the most recent had involved the Minnesota Civil Liberties Union.

The year Boni, our youngest, graduated from Kennedy High School, the graduating committee invited me to give the invocation. I was the only local pastor who had a child graduating that year.

But the MCLU decided to make this particular graduation prayer a test case. Kennedy, as a nationally recognized school, and Bloomington, as a highly visible community, would make for plenty of publicity—exactly what they wanted.

I Will Get You Ready

They filed a lawsuit, asking the U.S. District Court to forbid the graduation ceremony unless and until the prayers were removed from the program. They complained that prayers at public school events violated the state and federal constitutions, saying, "It is clear that the purpose of including prayer and other religious ceremonies in the graduation exercises is to imbue and color those exercises with religious principles."

I received calls from the media, and some visited me in person, seeking a copy of the prayer I was planning to give at the graduation. It surprised them to discover that I didn't write out my prayers before giving them.

When the MCLU heard about this, a representative contacted me. "Certainly you've constructed a prayer by *now*!" he said in disbelief. He seemed quite frustrated that I wouldn't give him something to fight against.

I had always disliked conflict, and here I had been handed a plateful. These people were powerful, savvy, well educated—and they knew how to be intimidating. But God had gotten me ready for this conflict, through years of dealing with difficult situations through prayer. In spite of my inner dismay, my feet were planted on solid rock, and I knew it.

I was being honest when I told these people that my prayers were extemporaneous. I went on to explain that when I prayed, I didn't pray to an audience—I made my supplications to the heavenly Father. They didn't seem to understand!

Strangely enough, although the MCLU tried to get a last minute injunction to stop me from praying, they privately encouraged me not to back down. They wanted to make a test case of the Kennedy graduation.

When this matter came before the judge, he was surprised. He said something like, "Do you mean to tell me that you're trying to stop this man from saying something, before he even says it?"

The lawyers for the MCLU were chagrined. They knew that what the judge was talking about was called prior restraint, and was clearly unconstitutional.

On the night of June 4, 1980, a large audience gathered at Met Center in Bloomington to witness as 500 seniors had their graduation ceremonies. When I approached the microphone to lead the graduation prayer, I paused for a moment to take a breath. Suddenly the entire senior class, their parents and friends, all stood to their feet and began to applaud.

They were not really cheering for me. They were cheering the fact that they were free to have the kind of graduation ceremony they wanted, without interference from anyone.

After the ceremony, young people came to me thanking me for helping them with their graduation. That gave me a good feeling. The episode with the Minnesota Civil Liberties Union had been stressful, to say the least.

But when I presented my situation to the Lord, my spirit was filled with peace.

Some Battles You're Never Ready For

New challenges presented themselves during the last few years I pastored at Bloomington Assembly. There were the usual stresses, of course; finding good staff, and retaining them, is always a big concern. And when you deal with people, there are always difficulties; not the least of which were my own shortcomings!

But we had one very big problem with a church member in those years, which involved the courts. Many people were hurt by this, the church was divided, and I saw a personal friend turn into an enemy.

Family relationships were not always perfect, either. Raising children is never easy, and Marian and I had had our share of struggles in that area. Now that our four children were married, you would think that our worries were over—but in reality, I think we prayed for them more than ever!

Marian's father, James D. Menzie, died. And Marian, with no siblings, felt the full burden of sorting out his finances, selling the house, and helping her mother make the necessary decisions.

But one of the biggest challenges, and one I was not at all ready for, came when Marian's doctor told us that she had cancer.

19

Singing in the Dark

"But let all who take refuge in You be glad, let them ever sing for joy..."

Psalms 5:11a

Arvid: I felt numb.

Marian had enjoyed excellent health all her life, with no vices except for the usual Scandinavian one—lots of coffee. But now the doctor was telling us that she had a malignancy in her colon.

As I hung up the phone, I had one thought in my mind—to get to Marian and hold her.

Marian: This is the biggest shock of cancer—just to hear that you have it. Cancer is something that happens to other people, you think.

Arvid: Later on I would think about what this would mean, and how long she would live, but at the time all I could think about was comforting her. And then we prayed.

Whenever you turn to the Lord in prayer, it lightens the burden. You're talking to someone who, from the very beginning, knows the end result. There are really no surprises for Him; He knows what's going on, and how to help us through whatever comes. He loves us completely, so really it's a matter of trust.

Move, and I Will Move

We agreed that we wanted to call for the elders of the church to pray over Marian, anointing her with oil, as James 5:14 says to do. We decided to do it the very next Sunday, February 28th.

But then we remembered that the 35th anniversary of Bloomington Assembly was coming up. There was a big open house planned for March 12th, and a special service for the 13th.

Marian: I knew that there would be many people at the open house who would want to talk to us. They would have memories to share, and good times to talk about, and the focus would be on the church and all that had been accomplished.

But if people knew I had cancer, then a good part of the focus would shift to me. I didn't want that.

I knew that people would be concerned, and want to ask questions and let me know they were praying—and while this is wonderful on a one to one basis, I quailed inwardly at facing hundreds of people who knew about my cancer and wanted to ask questions and talk about it. I just didn't feel strong enough for that.

Arvid: We decided to wait to let people know. In the meantime, Marian was supposed to leave for a women's retreat at Lake Geneva that afternoon. She wasn't the speaker, but she was part of the leadership of the church, and was expected to go.

Marian: I wanted to go. I felt that mingling with other women, in an atmosphere of praise and worship, would help me face the future with God's strength.

Arvid: We had an appointment the following week, during which Dr. Neimer outlined our options. They were basically radiation and surgery. The surgery would be one of two options—the usual colostomy, or a new procedure called resectioning. Dr. Neimer was one of only two specialists in the Twin Cities who did resectioning, and he recommended it.

Marian: I was afraid of having a colostomy, so I was glad to follow his recommendation. But he let us know that resectioning was not always possible, and he'd find out for sure on the operating table.

We waited and prayed. The 35th anniversary weekend arrived, and the church had surprised Arvid by bringing in General Superintendent G. Raymond Carlson to speak, and also Minnesota District Superintendent Herman Rhode. After the service, we asked for these men, along with the elders of the church and other godly people in leadership, to meet with us in the prayer chapel. They anointed me with oil, and prayed for my healing.

Arvid: I told the doctor that we believed in healing and in prayer. We had no way of knowing if the Lord had healed Marian or not, but we had a vacation scheduled to Florida, and the doctor told us to go. Upon our return he wanted to do additional biopsies, to see if there had been a healing. If not, he would prepare Marian for surgery.

In Florida, Marian very much wanted to visit a cousin of hers who had terminal cancer. We did, and this brought home to us what we might be dealing with. We spent ten days vacationing, waiting on the Lord and pondering our circumstances.

Divine Healing—or Not?

In our thinking and talking, we faced the subject of divine healing head-on. We discovered that it was more difficult to believe for divine healing than it was for spiritual healing. I asked myself the question, "Why doesn't physical healing come as easily as spiritual healing?"

I know of no one who has sincerely asked for God's forgiveness, that was rejected. *"He is rich unto all who call"* (Romans 10:12b).

But it is different with divine healing. Everyone who sincerely asks for physical healing is not healed; I don't know the reason. By their own admission neither did healing evangelists Dr. Charles S. Price, Kathryn Kuhlman, or Roxanne Brandt. R.W. McAlister said, "Salvation and healing are both in the atonement, but they are dispensed differently."

I've preached divine healing for nearly 50 years, and have witnessed numerous miracles as we've prayed for the sick. I've also prayed for hundreds with seemingly no results.

Several times, I've been marvelously healed. Sometimes when I wasn't healed by divine miracle, I've been healed when a physician fixed my torn retina, or when a surgeon operated and removed my ruptured appendix. Our family, too, has had supernatural interventions a number of times when we were not even aware of a problem, but God's leading brought us in contact with a physician to save our lives.

I've preached messages on healing. But everybody knows it's easier to preach on something than to live it out in life!

I've preached on "Coping with Crisis." I've preached on "Acting Your Faith," and we've done that too. I've also preached on "Overcoming Giant Fear." Even though most of us aren't fearful people, there are fears that try to fill our minds with an unknown 'What if?'

I've also preached on the 11th chapter of Hebrews which teaches that it often takes more faith not to be delivered than it takes to be rescued. The first part of the chapter talks about different kinds of deliverance by faith, but the last part gives a list of godly people who died while believing they would be delivered.

Hebrews 11:36 says:

>*Still others had trials of mockings and scourgings, yes, and of chains and imprisonment. They were stoned, they were sawn in two, were tempted, were slain with the sword. They wandered about in sheep-skins and goatskins, being destitute, afflicted, tormented–of whom the world was not worthy. They wandered in deserts and mountains, in dens and caves of the earth. And all these, having obtained a good testimony through faith, did not receive the promise. God having provided something better for us, that they should not be made perfect apart from us.*

Verse 33 refers to people like Daniel, "*...who stopped the mouths of lions.*" But there were also thousands of Christians who were eaten by lions, while praying that God would save them.

So God's ways and reasons are beyond us–yet as Job once said, "*Though He slay me, yet will I trust Him.*" (Job 13:15) I will not stop preaching divine healing, and I will not stop praying for the sick, though all my prayers aren't answered in the way I'd wish.

Even Jesus, when He was on earth, didn't heal everyone.[9] So if people aren't healed when I pray for them, still I've done what God has

---

[9]John 5:1-8, for example; it can be safely assumed that Jesus did not heal everyone at the pool of Bethesda.

asked me to do; and I leave the responsibility with Him.

Arvid: After we came home from Florida, Marian went in for the biopsies, and the cancer was still there. She was hospitalized, and preparations for surgery included a chest x-ray. It showed a cloudy area on her lung. Further tests confirmed it; there was a small spot, the size of an olive, which they couldn't identify.

"This is a worrisome turn of events," the doctor told us. He cancelled the surgery, and scheduled a biopsy of the lung for the following morning. He gently told us that if the biopsy revealed that the cancer had spread to the lung, then surgery would no longer be an option; and instead of talking about a cure, they would speak simply of treatment.

That was a very low moment for me. I came close to despair. I didn't want to lose my life's partner so soon.

Before I went home, I prayed over Marian, and then took her face in my hands. "We're going to get through this together. The Lord is going to see us through."

She said, "I know!" That was faith's answer.

I shared the latest developments with my staff, and they called a special prayer meeting for Wednesday morning. The prayer chain also went into action, and Wednesday evening over 150 showed up at midweek service. I felt very encouraged by all the prayer support!

Marian: That was a very dark night for me.

But I had taken a song with me when I went into the hospital. I had memorized all four verses of *The Solid Rock*, and although I didn't have the strength to sing it out loud, it ran through and through my head. The second verse especially had great meaning for me:

> *When darkness veils His lovely face,*
> *I rest on His unchanging grace;*
> *In every high and stormy gale,*
> *My anchor holds within the veil.*
> *On Christ, the solid Rock, I stand–*
> *All other ground is sinking sand,*
> *All other ground is sinking sand.* [10]

---

[10]Mote, Edward, and Bradbury, William. *The Solid Rock*.

This song was a very great comfort to me. After all, it's based on scripture, and that means it's God's truth.

Arvid: My song was "Faith is the Victory". It's a little more warlike. We were in a battle with cancer, and we were also fighting against the darkness of fear and despair—one of Satan's great weapons. But faith, according to the sixth chapter of Ephesians, is a shield for our defense; and the word of God is a sword.

Singing in Faith

It isn't a secret—it's all through the Bible—but still many people don't understand the powerful, shielding faith that you can get from singing a simple song of praise. I had experienced this many years before when our third child, Lynne, was a baby and fighting for her life.

Marian had had problems in the pregnancy, and had traveled to Little Falls to consult with the doctor she'd come to trust through the births of Kathy and Doug. The doctor made the decision to induce labor a month early; which meant that, instead of being present at the birth as I had planned, I was now stuck in the Twin Cities in the middle of a series of revival meetings!

Matters were made much worse when, at birth, Lynne's lungs failed to aerate properly. Marian called me, saying that the doctor had told her they didn't have the necessary equipment or expertise in Little Falls to deal with this emergency. So Calvin Scherling, a responsible young man I knew in Little Falls, sped Marian, the baby, and a nurse (who gave Lynne oxygen in the back seat) the hundred miles to Minneapolis in his car.

As I hung up the phone, I knew there wasn't a thing I could do but pray. And as I drove through traffic to meet them at the hospital, I found myself crying out to God in song:

> "*In life's dark and bitter hour, love will still prevail;*
> *Trust His everlasting pow'r, Jesus will not fail.*
> *Jesus never fails, Jesus never fails;*
> *Heav'n and earth may pass away, but Jesus never fails.*"[11]

---

[11] Luther, Arthur A. *Jesus Never Fails.*

Singing in the Dark

I sang this song and others like it, over and over, and my faith was strengthened. And I kept singing it through the next few months, for although Lynne survived that crisis, she was still weak and had a blue tinge to her skin. I'll never forget the day, a few months later, when she stopped breathing and went suddenly limp in my arms. In my panic I cried out to God.

A lot can go through your mind in a moment of crisis. I remember the sudden stabbing prayer sent up in a heartbeat, and a vow made all in a moment—"Lord, I'll do anything You want me to do, just save this child!"

All at once I felt impressed to hit her. I smacked her hard between the shoulder blades. She gave a little gasp, and began breathing again—and I was back to singing "Jesus Never Fails" in my mind, as we raced once more to the hospital.

Lynne did survive that bout (and several others) with pneumonia, and grew up to be a children's author, and is now helping me write this book! But at the time of my sung prayers, I did not know how things would turn out. I only knew this—that no matter what happened, Jesus truly would not fail me. And that song of faith helped build my faith and trust during a dark time.

David gives us a clue to this in the Psalms. Over and over, as he is faced with an enemy that is too great for him, he resorts to praise and thanksgiving in song. The 27th Psalm is just one of many, and says in part:

"For in the day of trouble He will conceal me in His tabernacle; in the secret place of His tent He will hide me... And I will offer in His tent sacrifices with shouts of joy; I will sing, yes, I will sing praises to the Lord." (NASB)

There are stories from the history of the Assemblies of God that reflect this wisdom, also.

In 1927, when F. J. Lindquist walked over acres of land that were for sale on the shores of Lake Geneva, he envisioned developing a Bible camp there, where people could come away from their heavy duties and spend time drawing near to God, and seeking His will for their lives.

He knew there would be obstacles. There were some who objected, saying "It costs too much—who will pay for it?" and "We don't have enough churches in our district to assume such a vision."

But in the face of all the obstacles, Brother Lindquist began to sing. As he walked, he sang; and as he sang, his faith grew. And Lake Geneva Bible Camp did come into being, and today is still thriving as Lake Geneva Christian Center.

I remember sitting under F. J. Lindquist's teaching when he was president of North Central Bible Institute. He often referred to the difficulties they faced when starting the Institute. When the situation seemed hopeless, the founders often broke out into singing praises to God—and God always came to their rescue!

When things seem hopeless, and you don't know what to do, you can begin singing a song in faith for God's intervention. You don't need to have voice lessons for this kind of singing. You don't need to know how to read music, or know the difference between soprano, alto, tenor or bass. You can be tone deaf, for all God cares! The music of our heart is what He listens to.

Singing in the Spirit

In Ephesians 5:18, Paul writes: *"Be not drunk with wine, in which is dissipation; but be filled with the Spirit, speaking to one another in psalms and hymns and spiritual songs, singing and making melody in your heart to the Lord."*

This verse is in the imperative mood; it's a command, not just a suggestion. And the significant thing about the command is that it's in the present tense, which in the Greek means 'in continuum', or always ongoing. It could be translated as "Keep on being filled with the Spirit."

There's much more to the Spirit-filled life than just a one time experience when we spoke in tongues, just as there is much more to physical nourishment than eating one very good breakfast. The energy we receive from the breakfast will soon be used up. It has to be replenished by more food later in the day.

There are thousands of believers who have an experience of the Holy Spirit that is valid, but they do not live in the fullness of the Spirit.

Singing in the Dark

The amazing thing is, it is very easy to keep being filled with the Holy Spirit—and Ephesians 5:19 tells us how. It specifically says we do it by "singing psalms, hymns, and spiritual songs."

That seems too simple; but it shouldn't surprise us. God's redemptive plan shows us that God has done all the difficult things; all we need to do is believe, and receive His provisions.

So what, exactly, is the difference between psalms, hymns, and spiritual songs?

I'd say that psalms are simply scriptures set to music. Some examples that we sing in our churches today are *Thy Loving Kindness (is Better Than Life)*[12] and *Seek Ye First (the Kingdom of God)*[13].

Hymns are often based upon scripture, but are written in the author's own words, and are used to teach truth and assist in praise. John Newton's *Amazing Grace* and Stuart Hine's *How Great Thou Art* are examples of hymns. I personally believe we need to be singing more hymns today; the great doctrines that teach the truths of God need to be rediscovered in the singing of this generation.

And spiritual songs are born in a person's heart by the Holy Spirit. You might be driving, or working around the house or yard, and just begin praising God in your own words, to your own tune or someone else's. Or you might begin singing in the language of the Spirit, one that you do not know. Paul speaks about both ways in 1 Corinthians 14:15 when he says, *"I will sing with the Spirit, and I will also sing with the understanding."*

This kind of singing is a strong shield against the Enemy, as I discovered one day a few years before Marian got cancer.

The church had been going through a difficult time, and I felt a real spirit of depression come over me. I felt it had also come over the congregation. Weeks passed, and the hindering of Satan had taken control, so that we were not experiencing the freedom of the Spirit in the church as we had experienced it several months back.

I prayed about it in desperation one day as I was walking through the empty sanctuary. I still remember exactly which aisle I was in.

---

[12] Mitchell, Hugh. *Thy Loving Kindness*. Based on Psalm 63:3,4.
[13] Lafferty, Karen. *Seek Ye First*. Based on Matthew 6:33; 7:7.

Suddenly I felt led to defy the spirit that seemed to hover like a black cloud over our church, by lifting my voice and singing in tongues.

No one was anywhere around as I walked up and down the aisles, singing in the Spirit. And as I continued, that spirit of depression lifted not only from me, but as I discovered later, it also left the congregation. From that moment on, God's Spirit began to work mightily in the services again.

No wonder that a few years later Marian and I both sang in response to fear and depression!

God's Loving Response

As Marian and I sang, through that long dark night after the shadow on her lung was discovered, God's Spirit was also working on our behalf—as we discovered the next morning.

Clarence St. John (currently the Minnesota District Superintendent, but at that time senior pastor of the Assemblies of God church in Hibbing) was having his regular devotional time that morning, when suddenly he received a strong message from God to pray for Marian.

He prayed for her, not knowing what was the matter. He had not heard of her cancer, and did not know she was in the hospital. After prayer, he attempted to call Marian, to tell her what had happened.

He was unable to reach her at home, and the church secretary, trying to protect our privacy, would give him no information. He persisted, and managed to put enough pressure on so that someone gave him the information he needed. At last he got through to Marian in her hospital room.

Marian: I picked up the phone, and Clarence said, "While I was in prayer this morning, the Lord laid a heavy burden on my heart for you. It felt urgent, but there was no particular message—just to pray for Marian."

Even today, I can't tell this story without tears coming to my eyes. The wonderful thing about his call was this: it told me that God knew where I was.

Arvid: That brought tears of joy to both of us; it was assurance that God was at work.

Something else happened which was extremely unusual. Just minutes after we checked Marian into her hospital room, a lovely young nurse walked in and said, "Hello, Pastor Kingsriter, I'm Marian's nurse tonight." I asked, "How do you know that I'm a pastor?" and she said, "I go to your church."

Well, if that wasn't something to rejoice over, about thirty minutes later another nurse came in to extract three tubes of blood, and wouldn't you know, she was also from our church, and sang in the choir.

The next afternoon the wife of one of our elders walked in and said to Marian, "I'm your nurse for tonight." And when I told the surgeon about these three nurses from our church, he said, "You've got them all over the place! I just met another one downstairs, and she asked me how Marian was getting along."

God knew our need and He bent over backwards to encourage us!

Marian: I was apprehensive about the biopsy. They use an exceedingly long needle, with no anesthetic, and stick it in your back all the way to your lung while you hold your breath.

So that song, *The Solid Rock*, was going through my mind again as the doctor stuck the needle in. He pulled it out, and said "There's no cancer there." He stuck it in again—no cancer—and again—no cancer.

The radiologist said the tissue from the lung didn't look malignant at all—but he thought that the shadowed spot might be tuberculosis. I was put in isolation, and Arvid had to wear a mask when he visited me, because I was now considered a public menace!

But when the results came back from the Board of Health, it turned out to be a fungal infection, common in the Mississippi Valley, and nothing to be concerned about.

This was another occasion for praise and thanksgiving! But now I was facing the actual surgery. Dr. Neimer came in with a marker and said, "If I end up having to do a colostomy, where do you want the opening?"

Oh, I was fearful. I said, "I don't *want* a colostomy!"

He gently explained that he hoped to do the resectioning we had talked about, but if I was on the operating table and it turned out to be impossible, he wouldn't be able to wake me up to ask where I wanted the colostomy.

So he put a mark on my body for that opening, and I went into the surgery, not knowing what would happen. And in my mind I had moved on to the third verse:

> His oath, His covenant, His blood,
> Support me in the whelming flood;
> When all around my soul gives way,
> He then is all my hope and stay.[14]

We had prayed for divine healing, and God had not answered that prayer in the way we had hoped. But I still had reason to be thankful. I was in the hands of a wonderful surgeon; and better than that, no matter what happened, I knew I was in the hands of God, and that I was His child.

Arvid: We knew of two ways the cancer could be cured: divine healing and by medical means. Regarding divine healing, we obeyed everything we knew to do that the Scriptures teach.

I know that there are some who preach, "Don't go to a doctor, believe only." Some of those people are no longer with us. In saying this, I'm not faulting their decision.

Marian and I decided go both routes. We decided to believe God for divine healing, for all healing comes from God—and to also ask the medical profession to help the process.

Once in awhile I'll run into someone who is confused about the subject of healing. They think God's only work is in the realm of the supernatural, and that somehow the devil gets involved in medicine.

God clearly does not limit himself to work only through what we would call supernatural, because the Bible and our own experience has shown, over and over again, that He loves to work through people.

Furthermore, I can just about guarantee that the devil is not involved in medicine, because he wouldn't do anything to make anybody feel better. You can count on that! So medical help is just another expression of God's mercy to mankind.

We prayed for Marian—in fact, there were thousands of people who prayed for her—and further tests did not reveal that there had been a healing. So we accepted that God's answer was "No", and we scheduled the surgery.

Today, at this writing, Marian is still by my side. The doctor did not

[14] Mote, Edward, and Bradbury, William. *The Solid Rock.*

Singing in the Dark

have to perform a colostomy, and she has been cancer free for seventeen years; all glory and praise to God, who provided medical help when we needed it.

This is not a jaw-dropping story of miraculous healing. This is just a tale of one ordinary couple in Christ, fumbling through and learning first-hand what it means to live out the word of God.

We learned that even when God doesn't miraculously intervene, He still lovingly watches over us. He encouraged us through His people—through a phone call at just the right time, through caring and godly nurses, through the skill of a surgeon, through the thousands of people who sent letters and prayed.

And even beyond, God encouraged us through people like Edward Mote and William Bradbury, John Yates and Ira D. Sankey—men long dead, but whose words and music reflected the faith by which they lived and died, the faith to which we clung when all seemed dark.

> *To him that overcomes the foe,*
> *White raiment shall be giv'n;*
> *Before the angels he shall know*
> *His name confessed in heav'n.*
> *Then onward from the hills of light,*
> *Our hearts with love aflame,*
> *We'll vanquish all the hosts of night,*
> *In Jesus' conquering name.*
> *Faith is the victory! Faith is the victory!*
> *Oh, glorious victory, that overcomes the world.*[15]

---

[15]Yates, John, and Sankey, Ira. *Faith is the Victory.*

Move, and I Will Move

20

Changing of the Guard

"'For I know the plans I have for you,' declares the Lord; '...plans to give you a future and a hope.'"
Jeremiah 29:11-13 (NASB)

I blinked my eyes to clear my vision. Still cloudy.

I shut off the alarm and looked over at Marian, who was just waking up. Her outline was blurred and dark, and at the same time oddly clear in spots—I couldn't make sense of what I was seeing.

I closed one eye, then the other. That showed me the problem. The right eye had gone bad, somehow, in the night, and my brain was having trouble putting the images from both eyes together.

I almost groaned aloud. Whatever was the matter with my eye would have to wait. It was Sunday morning, and I had services to conduct. But how I would read my sermon notes, I didn't know.

"Please, God, just help me get through today," I prayed.

With great difficulty, I stumbled through my sermon, and an evening service too. But that night I was beat. And I thought again with longing of the day when I would be able to pass my responsibilities on to someone else.

Just one year before, shortly after Marian had been diagnosed with cancer, I had told my staff that I planned to retire. I met with the church board, the elders, and my entire staff, and took them point by point through a document outlining the steps they needed to take to find a replacement for me.

"I want to retire soon," I said. "I will stay until you find a replacement—but I'd like you to accomplish this as soon as possible, and within two years at the most."

I was in my 68th year, after all, and I was still working at full throttle. Besides being the senior pastor for Bloomington Assembly of God, I was also the assistant district superintendent. I found myself wondering if I would ever be able to enjoy some free time!

Oh, I took breaks each day, and the church had sent us on several wonderful trips. But my focus was always on my work. I visited other churches, always with an eye out for what they were doing, what was working, and new ideas that we could incorporate at Bloomington Assembly. We went overseas to visit our missionaries, and encourage them. It was thrilling to go on these trips, and see the fruit of the seeds our church had helped plant; but even on vacations my mind was always working.

I wanted relief from that constant pressure of having to think, to plan, to produce, to excel. Also, there were many things I had wanted to do, which I had set aside. I told myself, "You can get along without that," and I had.

But when Marian was diagnosed with cancer, I decided I didn't want to put things off any longer. And so I had tried to prepare the church leadership for the task of finding my replacement.

Nearly a year had gone by, with little progress on that front. There was no new pastor waiting in the wings. And now, suddenly, I had a major problem with my eyes.

I went to the doctor, and he diagnosed an occlusion. Blood had pooled in my eye, and wasn't able to get out.

"Sometimes these things clear up in a week or two," he said. "But I can't promise you anything."

Of course we prayed. And I kept trying to work as we waited to see if the problem would resolve itself. But I couldn't read or study well at all—a serious handicap when preparing sermons!

Some pastors, I am told, have an easy time with their sermons. They just get up and speak extemporaneously, without having to work at it. I was never like that. It takes me much longer to prepare than the average person.

Perhaps part of the reason is that I never finished high school. I did eventually go to college, and graduate from North Central Bible Institute, but I always felt that those missing three years of high school were a handicap for me. I recognized my lack of education, and as a result always worked harder to try to make up for it.

There was another reason why it took me a long time to prepare sermons. I felt strongly that, whenever I spoke, it was essential that I speak under the power and anointing of the Holy Spirit. If at all possible, I would take two to three days to myself each week, just to read and study and pray and prepare. I wanted to take plenty of time to meet with God, and see what He wanted to say through me.

When I felt filled with the Holy Spirit, filled with the message I had been given, then I was glad and eager to preach. But if, for one reason or another, I hadn't been able to spend the necessary time in prayer and study, then giving a sermon was torture.

Now I had a new challenge in preparing sermons. The vision problem I was experiencing not only made it hard to read, but seemed to affect my comprehension as well. I couldn't focus; I would forget what I had read just moments before. It was frustrating. And to make matters worse, my bad eyes affected my ability to play sports.

All my life, I had used sports to keep myself mentally and physically energized. Golf, tennis, handball—it didn't matter. As long as there was a ball involved, and I could hit it, I was happy. It was a way to keep fit and work off stress at the same time.

But now, with no depth perception, I kept missing the ball. Sports, that had once been my refuge, were now just one more source of frustration. And when the occlusion didn't clear up after a couple of weeks, I realized that the problem wasn't going away.

I started to develop the attitude that I was going to have to live with it, so there was no use complaining! But at the next board meeting, I told those assembled that it was time to step up the search for a replacement for me.

"This eye problem has slowed me down," I said, "and I don't feel I can keep on much longer. I will stay as long as I can, but you need to find a new senior pastor—soon."

I asked that they form a search committee, and suggested three couples who, I thought, would make a good team for that purpose. I gave them some ground rules to consider, and urged them to begin immediately. The board voted to approve my suggestions, and the ball was finally rolling.

Getting Out and Staying Out

Changing senior pastors is difficult for any church. The transition is harder if the outgoing pastor has been around a long time—and even worse if he is also the founding pastor.

A church that has only had one senior pastor gets to think that there is only one right way to do things, and that is the way the real pastor did it! As a result, the man who succeeds him often has a very tough time of it.

Historically, in cases like this, the new pastor tends to last only a year or two, becoming essentially an interim pastor. This is a hurtful and often divisive situation for both pastor and church.

I knew this, and it concerned me deeply. I decided that I would do everything in my power to assure that this tragedy did not happen to Bloomington Assembly, and to its future senior pastor. I thought about it, and prayed about it. I created a plan for transition that I hoped would smooth the process.

And then I prepared myself to get out of the way.

The first thing I did was to back off from the search committee and the board's decisions. I realized early on that I would have to do this, when Jerry Strandquist's name was mentioned as a possible replacement for me.

Jerry was senior pastor of a thriving church in Kenosha, Wisconsin. He was also my son-in-law, married to my daughter Kathy. Secretly, in my heart, I was happy that the board was considering his name. But I didn't want there to be any taint of nepotism. Besides, this was God's church, not Arvid Kingsriter's. I decided that if God wanted Jerry to be my successor, then He could work without my interfering!

So every time Jerry's name came up for discussion I excused myself, so that the board could discuss him freely, and make the decisions they wanted to make.

I was present for the search committee's reports on other potential pastors. Sometimes I would know something about the pastor under discussion, but for reasons of confidentiality couldn't share it. In that case I would just say "I don't think he would be a very good choice." But mostly I just listened.

They had a whole list of names, but Jerry Strandquist was the first one they visited. After they interviewed him in Kenosha, they said "We think you're our guy." But Jerry asked them to look at the other names on the list first.

To make a long story short, in the end they came back to Jerry and said, in effect, "We still think you're our guy." He and Kathy, after going through the candidate process, were recommended by the board and search committee, elected by the congregation, and accepted the call to come to Bloomington Assembly.

I retired in November, 1989. I was full of joy on that day—joy that I was retiring at last, joy that the church had a wonderful, energetic new pastor to guide and guard it in the years to come.

But I had one more thing to do. I had to walk out the door, and stay out.

Instructions To the Church
Keep Looking to Christ

On November 12, 1989, I preached my farewell message at Bloomington Assembly of God, which I had pioneered almost thirty-seven years earlier. It was the last of several messages preparing the congregation for transition to their new pastor.

My text that day was 1 Corinthians 3:4-9. This passage gave a biblical background for what I was going to say in my farewell to this congregation whom I loved so much.

> *For when one says, 'I am of Paul' and another, 'I am of Apollos' are you not carnal?' (Or to paraphrase, 'When one says, 'I am of Kingsriter,' and another, 'I am of Strandquist,' are you not carnal?) Who then is Paul, and who is Apollos, but ministers through whom*

you believed, as the Lord gave to each one? I planted, Apollos watered, but God gave the increase. So then neither he who plants is anything, nor he who waters, but God who gives the increase. Now he who plants and he who waters are one, and each one will receive his own reward according to his own labor. For we are God's fellow workers; you are God's field, you are God's building.

I went on to say, "This congregation is not of Arvid Kingsriter. You are of God. Your faith isn't built upon a personality. It must be built upon Christ. If your faith is built upon a man you have a wrong and unscriptural object for your faith. You are of Christ, beloved. So as I leave and your new pastor comes, keep looking to Christ, because He is '...*the author and finisher of our faith.*' "[16]

Our Relationship Must Change

I told the congregation how much being their pastor had meant to me. I told them that their new pastor had requested that Marian and I continue worshipping at Bloomington Assembly, and remain active participants in the church.

I also told them that this was not going to happen.

One reason I gave was this: I felt called to start a mentoring program. In this work, I planned to go from church to church, studying the strengths and weaknesses of young, beginning pastors, with an eye to pairing them with retired, experienced pastors.

But the deeper reason was this—*I was no longer their pastor.* They needed to make the switch, and if Marian and I were still around, that process could be sidetracked.

We felt it would be better, at least for a period of time, for us to attend church elsewhere. We wanted to give the congregation the best possible chance to develop a relationship with their new pastor and his wife. Sometimes a clean break is best!

So I spoke plainly. "Marian and I want to remain your friends forever. But after November 28th, you will need to transfer pastoral responsibilities to the new pastor. This is the right thing to do. So please

---

[16]Hebrews 12:2.

don't call on me to perform any pastoral duties such as baby dedications, weddings, or funerals. If you want me to conduct your funeral, I'll have to do it in the next ten days."

This got a laugh, but I was serious! And, looking back, I think it was one of the smartest things I have ever done.

Stay United

I spoke to the congregation that morning as if I were a father, leaving instructions and practical advice for future behavior. Along with expressing my love, gratitude, and thanksgiving for this wonderful body of people, I reminded them that they had made their choice of the Strandquists, and gave this clear warning:

"If you want me to get really upset, I think it would happen if I heard that after a congregation has prayed and sought the face of God for guidance, and then voted in the man they felt God wanted for a church, they later second-guessed and wondered if they'd gotten the right one.

"Listen, your new pastor will go through a tremendous process of accepting the call of God for this church, and part of that process is you. When the church has made its choice there's no point in any of you saying: 'Well, I didn't vote for him.' You are a part of this body, and the moment there is a two-thirds vote you speak with one voice, and you say, 'He's my pastor.' And that has nothing to do with whether you voted for him or not, or even if you were present at the membership meeting. You were part of the process, and you're a part spiritually of this body, and this body must stay united.

"And I'm not going to criticize, but you can count on me to cooperate."

Accept Your New Pastor

"Surveys reveal," I said, "that it takes a new pastor at least five years to feel accepted. A new pastor is like a heart transplant. He is transplanted into your body (to replace the old heart that's worn out), but it's your body that decides whether to accept or reject that transplant. Now, the life of the church is Jesus Christ; He is the life-source, but the function is in the pastor. As his heart beats, as his vision is seen, as his life is lived, the whole church moves ahead.

"The history of churches with long-term founding pastors shows that it's extremely difficult for the pastor who succeeds him. You people hold the key...you can accept or reject this transplant. I pray that every one will do all that's in your power to make him and his family feel accepted genuinely and warmly as soon as possible."

Be Patient, and Expect Changes

"Another bit of advice is to be patient with him regarding remembering your name. Please don't anyone go up to him in two or three months and say: "I bet you don't remember my name." Well, how could he? There are over 2000 people who call this their church. I've been around for many years and I still don't know many of your names. So be patient. Give him time."

"Be patient with him, too, when he begins to make some changes. Give him a chance. He's going to be different, and you want to thank God for that.

"Furthermore, don't expect him to fill my shoes. I'm not going to leave my shoes here. He'll bring his own. When you hear people say. 'It's not the same,' remember that of course it won't be the same. He's going to want to make some changes that will fit his personality, and his temperament.

"Believe in him, allow him to make a few blunders, and be kind to him. Remember, I certainly didn't please all the people all the time, either!"

Pray for Your New Pastor

"Finally, pray for your new pastor, and encourage him. You have no idea how a little encouragement will make him a better pastor. There have been times when I've been down, wondering if my ministry was effective, and then I opened my mail and read something like – 'Pastor, you will never know how that message helped me, or how it changed my life,' and it made all the difference.

"If you treat your new pastor like you've treated me, he'll become one of the greatest pastors anywhere. Many years ago I went to preach in Calvary Temple, in Winnipeg, Manitoba, and just before I was to leave the little preparation room behind the stage, about six or seven strong men came in and said: 'We'd like to pray for you before you go into the service.' I said: 'Oh, please do.' So they gathered around me, laid hands on me and prayed. Dear ones, you have no idea what that did for me. I entered the service buoyed up in the Spirit, and preached with a precious anointing, and something like two dozen people responded to the altar call for salvation at the close."

Looking Back

There have been many changes at Bloomington Assembly in the past sixteen years. A new church, Oak Hills, was planted in Eagan and pastored by Rod Carlson, a man whose parents were charter members of Bloomington Assembly of God. An addition was built, a large atrium that serves as a multi-purpose meeting area. A missions house was purchased and furnished, missions giving went through the roof, and the name itself changed to Cedar Valley Church when Bloomington Assembly merged with Cedar Ridge Assembly. And the church just kept on growing, planting new seeds, tending the vigorous shoots, reaping the harvest and sowing again.

At this writing, it is more than sixteen years since the changing of the guard at Bloomington Assembly. I am grateful beyond measure to report that the transition went well, and that Jerry Strandquist is still senior pastor.

I can compliment the whole church for that. They let me go, and embraced the new pastor and his family in the most gracious manner. Of course at times people would run into me and say things like "It's so nice to see you, pastor, and we miss you," but not one person tried to speak negatively to me about how things were going, or told me that they were leaving the church!

And I didn't find fault either, though I have to confess that my staff had a guessing game about that. They were waiting to see how long it would take for me to return and complain that things weren't being done right. They are still waiting!

Move, and I Will Move

But while it is true that I let go of the reins of leadership, I still had a strong work ethic I needed to fulfill. And to be truly happy, I had to feel that my work mattered; I had to feel I was doing something to advance the kingdom of God.

But how to accomplish this, given the declining energy and capacity of old age?

21

Pressing On

"Brethren, I do not regard myself as having laid hold of it yet; but one thing I do: forgetting what lies behind and reaching forward to what lies ahead, I press on toward the goal for the prize of the upward call of God in Christ Jesus."

Philippians 3:13-14 (NASB)

Nearly 2,000 people lifted their voices in a powerful hymn, and I wept, standing before them. The words called me to account, for they were about the day when we'd all stand before our Lord to answer for how we'd lived our lives while here on earth.

Had I really done my best for the Lord? Had I taken advantage of all the opportunities that He'd given me? Thoughts like these flooded my mind as I looked out over the wonderful people of Bloomington Assembly during our farewell service.

I wasn't sure that I had. I knew that my motives hadn't gone unnoticed by God. I wondered how much of what I had done was prompted by a desire to achieve, and how much was done for the glory of God.

For days afterward I searched my heart in prayer, reflecting on this question: *What motivated me in doing the work of a shepherd?*

Whatever the answer, I knew that it was too late to make any changes in my ministry at Bloomington Assembly. Those opportunities were all in the past.

The Pressure is Off!

"Isn't this wonderful?" I said to Marian as we drove out the first Sunday morning of our retirement. "I don't have to preach. I'm not responsible for anything. Do you have any idea how good that feels?"

This was the best thing about retirement, for me: the lifting of the heavy burden of responsibility that I carried. The pressure had been intense, and it had been there day and night.

Admittedly, I put myself under much of that pressure. I have a big motor inside that has to be satisfied. I have a strong inner drive to succeed at whatever I am doing, and I don't like to fail.

Of course, a certain amount of failure is inevitable if you're going to launch out and take steps of faith. I learned to accept it and just keep on going.

But because of this drive within me, I was constantly thinking, planning, trying to learn how to do something better; my mind was never at rest. Even on vacation, while we were visiting other churches, I was always looking for ideas. What was working? What could we incorporate at Bloomington Assembly?

And there were some things I had given up. "You can get along without that," I had told myself, whenever a personal desire had conflicted with work pressures.

So now, with retirement, I savored some new joys:

The ability to spend relaxed time with Marian, doing little chores or errands together, just enjoying her companionship.

The chance to watch a ball game from *start to finish*, with no guilt!

And, best of all, to be able to go to church and simply worship in the presence of God, with no responsibilities and with my mind at rest.

And the Pressure is On Again

I have to admit that, amid the joys of retirement, I was still pretty busy.

I served another ten years as assistant district superintendent. Some of my assignments included developing a program for mentoring young pastors, and chairing a committee that addressed the problem of reconciliation in churches where bitterness and division have occurred.

Pressing On

I also traveled throughout the state, raising funds for a new retreat center at Lake Geneva.

I entered the computer age, and had to learn a whole new way of thinking. I needed all the help I could get! But the computer, a gift from Bloomington Assembly, has been a wonderful (if frustrating) tool in my continuing work.

As I ended my term as assistant to our district superintendent, Marian and I were given a new ministry—that of reaching out to the widows of Assemblies of God ministers and missionaries.

Ministerial widows not only lose their husbands, but also their pastors; and many of them must move away from the congregation where they had been in ministry, thereby losing their friends and support group as well. Many end up somewhat isolated, sad and lonely.

Our task was simple; we were to take these widows out to lunch for their birthdays, and present them with a check from the district as a birthday present. Marian added her own touch by bringing along candles for the dessert, and singing *Happy Birthday*.

Such a small thing, but it made such a big difference to these dear ladies. I was often reminded of James 1:27 which says, *"Pure and undefiled religion before God and the Father is this: to visit orphans and widows in their trouble..."* Later on we added visits to retired single women who had been in full time ministry; and I have to say that of all the pastoral experiences I've had throughout the years, this one has to rank near the top.

But as Marian and I got older, we had to slowly release all these tasks to younger people, to those with more vigor.

Loss Has a Purpose

Psalms 92:12-13 says, *"For the godly...are transplanted into the Lord's own garden, and are under His personal care."* (LB) I've taken trees from the woods and transplanted them in my garden because I wanted that tree close to me, so I could enjoy it. This is what God does with us, especially in old age.

Aging brings loss. This is inevitable.

Marian and I have buried our parents, my brothers, other family members, and many dear friends. We were once young and strong, but now we are dealing with the realities of aging bodies. There are very few left who remember us as we were in our youth.

King Solomon wrote a pretty accurate description of old age in Ecclesiastics 12 (The Message):

> *Honor and enjoy your Creator while you're still young,*
> *Before the years take their toll and your vigor wanes,*
> *Before your vision dims and the world blurs*
> *And the winter years keep you close to the fire.*
> *In old age, your body no longer serves you so well.*
> *Muscles slacken, grip weakens, joints stiffen.*
> *The shades are pulled down on the world.*
> *You can't come and go at will. Things grind to a halt.*
> *The hum of the household fades away.*
> *You are wakened now by bird-song.*
> *Hikes to the mountains are a thing of the past.*
> *Even a stroll down the road has its terrors.*
> *Your hair turns apple-blossom white,*
> *Adorning a fragile and impotent matchstick body.*
> *Yes, you're well on your way to eternal rest,*
> *While your friends make plans for your funeral.*
> *Life, lovely while it lasts, is soon over.*
> *Life as we know it, precious and beautiful, ends.*
> *The body is put back in the same ground it came from.*
> *The spirit returns to God, who first breathed it.*

The above passage gives us a realistic picture of what Paul meant in 2 Corinthians 4:16 when he said, *"The outward man is perishing."* But the remaining half of that verse says, *"...yet the inward man is being renewed day by day."*

God takes us gently away from the scene of our strength and youth, and transplants us into His garden. We become very close to Him as we lose everything else that was so important to us.

I can just hear someone saying, "But where the Lord has planted me doesn't look at all like a garden, and especially not the garden of God."

Pressing On

But did you ever see a tree standing all alone in some rocky place, under the blazing sun, with no lake or river in sight, and yet its leaves were green? The vegetation around it was burned and dead, but the tree not only survived; it was flourishing.

What was its secret? Just this: down deep under the soil, there flowed an underground stream that nourished the tree. The vegetation around it did not have roots deep enough to reach the water. But the tree's roots were deep and well established, and reached down to the source of its life.

God may have planted some of us in what seems to be a dry place, but our roots are deep, and we are drawing from the hidden streams of His grace and love. And this not only makes us green and flourishing in our old age, but also enables us to still bear fruit.

The verses following Psalms 92:13 make that clear: *"Even in old age they will still produce fruit and be vital and green. This honors the Lord, and exhibits His faithful care. He is my shelter. There is nothing but goodness in Him!"* (LB)

The true secret to setting our roots deep into life-giving water, and still bearing fruit in old age, is found in an active relationship with God through His indwelling Spirit. Whatever our age, we can overlook some things, but we can never afford to neglect our prayer life. If prayer and genuine communion with God is the only thing we make sure to do on a daily basis, we will still accomplish much more than if we fill our lives with busy activities, but have no time for Him.

When we do that, we find that our attitude is transformed! Instead of feeling bitter about the inevitable changes and difficulties of our lives, we become truly grateful for all we have been given.

And in the end, of course, no matter how heavy the burdens and pressures of responsibility, no matter how painful the indignities and weakness of age, these sorrows are all fleeting. We shall be changed! Paul reminds us in 1 Corinthians 15 that while our bodies now are weak, they shall be raised in power; and although they were sown in dishonor, they shall be raised in glory. This is a blessed hope!

Move, and I Will Move

God Loves to Use Weak People

Had I really done my best for the Lord? Had I taken advantage of all the opportunities that He'd given me? What had motivated me in doing the work of a shepherd?

These questions that haunted me, during the farewell service and after my retirement, had simple answers. No, I hadn't done my best at all times. I hadn't taken advantage of every opportunity given me, and my motivation in doing the work of God was not 100% for His glory. Although some people in my life have tried to put me on a pedestal, I don't belong there. I am weak, I am fallible, and my proper place is at the foot of the cross with all the other sinners.

But God's grace was present even in my weakness, for which I shall be eternally grateful.

Being a pastor has been a privilege, given by God to an undeserving servant. My greatest thrill in life has been watching the Great Church Builder at work. Looking back, there were times I couldn't see where God was taking us, nor could I hear His voice saying: "This is the way, walk in it."

But I could trust that He was always at work. His patience with me and His blessing upon my life have been much more than I deserved, or ever dreamed possible.

All glory be to God!

†